MORE
VERTICAL QUILTS
with
S·T·Y·L·E

BOBBIE A. AUG & SHARON NEWMAN

American Quilter's Society

P. O. Box 3290 • Paducah, KY 42002-3290

www.AQSquilt.com

Located in Paducah, Kentucky, the American Quilter's Society (AQS) is dedicated to promoting the accomplishments of today's quilters. Through its publications and events, AQS strives to honor today's quiltmakers and their work and to inspire future creativity and innovation in quiltmaking.

EDITOR: SHELLEY HAWKINS
GRAPHIC DESIGN: LYNDA SMITH
COVER DESIGN: MICHAEL BUCKINGHAM
PHOTOGRAPHY: CHARLES R. LYNCH

Library of Congress Cataloging-in-Publication Data
Aug, Bobbie A.
   More vertical quilts with style / by Bobbie A. Aug and Sharon Newman.
      p. cm.
Continues: Vertical quilts with style.
   ISBN 1-57432-777-1
  1. Patchwork--Patterns. 2. Quilting--Patterns. I. Newman, Sharon,
1942- II. Aug, Bobbie A. Vertical quilts with style. III Title.
   TT835 .a94 2002
     746.46'041--dc21

                         2001004935

Additional copies of this book may be ordered from the American Quilter's Society, PO Box 3290, Paducah, KY 42002-3290, or online at www.AQSquilt.com.

Dedication

We dedicate this book to our husbands, Norm Aug and Tommy Newman, for encouraging us to pursue our love of quiltmaking any way we can! We also dedicate it to each of our children for having to grow up with quilters' pins on the carpet and threads on their clothes. A special dedication goes to their families who have come to accept that their mother-in-law or grandmother, whichever the case, will always be knee-deep in fabric scraps and manuscripts.

Our children and their families:

Anthony (Tony) E. Aug
Carrie (Sis) A. Aug
Tifani Adams Aug
Tracy Newman Faulkner
Todd Faulkner
Clinton Thomas Faulkner
Taylor Alexandra Faulkner
Vicki Newman Potts
Gary Potts
Amanda Lea Potts
Sarah Jolene Potts
Carol Newman Gilson, M.D.
Wes Gilson
Emily Katherine Gilson

Acknowledgments

We express our gratitude to Meredith Schroeder for publishing this second book on vertical quilts, thereby giving us the opportunity to continue our addiction to making them.

A special thanks goes to our good friend, Gerald E. Roy, for his continued friendship and support. We also wish to thank Sandi Freuhling, Glendora Hutson, and Richard Cleveland for their friendship and special talents. We appreciate the ongoing support from Anne Brann, and Ann and Rex Porter.

Contents

INTRODUCTION

In *Vertical Quilts with Style*, our first book on this time-honored technique, we patterned many of the traditional designs from the nineteenth century. The study of quilts made during the first hundred years of this country's history reveals the richness of the variety in design and style, as well as the increasing abundance of fabric. We had a great time making those quilts.

Twentieth-century quiltmakers have long used these traditional patterns, styles, and quilting designs in evolving changes incorporating new fabric technologies. Upon reviewing our quilt and quilt top collections, slides, and pictures accumulated during our research, we discovered many new designs, color schemes, and variations on this distinctive set. We couldn't wait to make more vertical quilts, using up-to-date sewing techniques and fabrics. The quilts featured in this supplement to *Vertical Quilts with Style* are fun and easy. Showing others how the vertical settings change even the simplest designs brought us excitement and satisfaction.

Come along and experience the joy of transforming a few easy blocks into stunning quilts.

GENERAL INSTRUCTIONS

Read through the following information before you begin your quilting project.

IMPORTANT TIPS

- Wash and press fabric before measuring and cutting.
- Remove selvages from the fabric.
- Use a ¼" seam allowance throughout. Sew 10 to 12 stitches per inch.
- Be as accurate as possible in your measuring, cutting, and sewing. A .5 mechanical pencil will keep your lines consistent. Acrylic rulers, 6" x 24", are helpful when cutting long sashing strips and borders.
- Generally, press seam allowances toward the darker fabric with the iron on the cotton setting. We prefer steam, but use caution when pressing bias edges. Place patchwork dark side up on your ironing board. Press the seam first to set it and also to flatten any puckers in the stitching. Gently lift the dark fabric and let the iron push it back over the seam allowance. Do not pull on the fabric, which could cause stretching. The key is to press, not iron.

Press seam to set it.

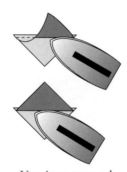

Use iron to push top triangle back.

SETTING BLOCKS ON POINT (CHART, PAGE 11)

Many vertical quilts feature pieced blocks set on point. This arrangement of blocks requires the use of side and corner setting triangles. To find the size squares you will need to cut to make the setting triangles, you need to know the diagonal measurements of your blocks. To find the diagonal, multiply the finished block size by 1.414.

SIDE AND CORNER TRIANGLES (CHART, PAGE 12)

The size of the square to cut for the corner triangles is half the diagonal measurement of the finished block plus ⅞". Cut two squares once diagonally to make four corners.

The size of the square to cut for the side triangles is the diagonal measurement of the finished block plus 1¼". Cut one square twice diagonally to make four side triangles.

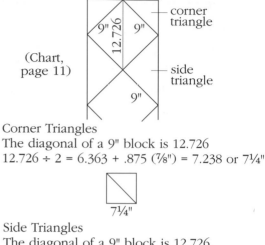

(Chart, page 11)

Corner Triangles
The diagonal of a 9" block is 12.726
$12.726 \div 2 = 6.363 + .875 (⅞") = 7.238$ or 7¼"

7¼"

Side Triangles
The diagonal of a 9" block is 12.726.
$12.726 + 1.25 = 13.976$ or 14"

14"

MAKING HALF-SQUARE TRIANGLE UNITS

These units contain squares made from two contrasting half-square triangles. The short sides of the triangles are on the straight grain of fabric and the long sides are on the bias.

The simplest way to sew the unit is to cut two triangles of appropriate size. Place them right sides together and stitch along the long side. Open and press.

Matching the points accurately can be difficult. Please refer to the Resources section, page 95, for a list of tools that will help form accurate half-square triangle units.

QUILT BORDERS

Lay the quilt top on a flat surface and use a tape measure to determine the length of the quilt through the center and each side of the quilt top. The two outer measurements should be the same as the center measurement.

ADDING BORDERS WITH STRAIGHT CORNERS

The two border strips should be cut to match the measured length. Fold the quilt top in half and mark the center of each side of the quilt with pins. Fold in half again and mark the fourths, then fold again and mark the eighths. Fold and mark the centers, quarters, and eighths of the border strips in the same fashion.

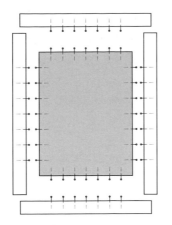

Match the pins as you pin the side borders to the quilt top. As you stitch each border, add more pins between the divisions as necessary. Sew with the border strips on top, because they are more stable than the pieced quilt top. Press.

To add the top and bottom borders, measure the width of the quilt top through the center and across the top and bottom, including the side borders. Cut border strips to this measurement. Attach the border strips to the quilt top and bottom edges.

ADDING BORDERS WITH MITERED CORNERS
The two border strips should be cut to the measured length plus two finished border widths, plus seam allowances, plus 2" to 3" for extra mitering length.

Refer to "Adding Borders with Straight Corners" for measuring and pinning borders.

Pin each border strip to the quilt top, matching center, quarter, and eighth marks. Start and end your stitching ¼" from the corners of the quilt. Sew the four borders to the quilt top, backstitching at each starting and stopping point.

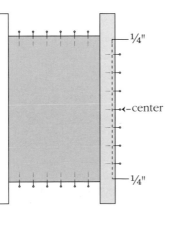

As you sew each border, add more pins between the divisions as necessary. Sew with the border strips on

top, because they are more stable than the pieced quilt top. Ease in any fullness. Press.

Once the borders are added, miter the corners. Fold the corner, right sides together, aligning the side edge with the top edge exactly. Begin stitching at the end of the seam line ¼" from the corner, following the angle of the fold. Sew to the edge of the outer border.

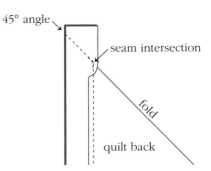

Turn to the right side, open the corner, and press. Trim seam allowance to ¼". Repeat for remaining corners.

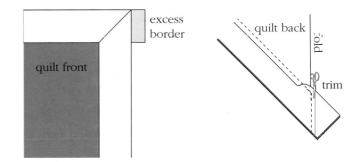

PREPARING FOR QUILTING

PLANNING THE QUILTING DESIGN

Whether you machine or hand quilt your project may influence your choice of quilting designs. Diagonal lines, grids, and parallel lines are popular background patterns. Mark the fabric with a pencil and ruler, or use masking tape as a guide. Free-motion machine stippling is another popular background design. Wreaths, feathers, cables, and baskets enhance open spaces. Many of these designs are available in commercial stencils and pattern books. However, it can be fun to use personalized motifs and symbols in an original design.

The quantity of quilting should be adequate to hold the batting in place. Whichever designs you choose, plan them on the quilt's surface before marking.

MARKING THE QUILTING DESIGN

Thoroughly press the quilt top, making sure all seam allowances lie flat. Test your pencils or markers on scraps of quilt fabrics to make sure you can remove the marks later.

A non-skid surface, such as a rotary cutting mat, is great to use under your quilt top when marking to eliminate "drag" and fabric slippage. Begin marking wherever you like; however, borders should be marked from the corners to the center of each side to allow for any adjustments needed in the border pattern repeat.

CHOOSING BATTING

Choose the batting thickness and fiber content desired for your quilt. Batting comes in a variety of fibers including cotton, polyester, cotton and poly-ester blends, silk, and wool. Some are easier to quilt through than others. The most important factor in choosing a batting is the quality of the product. Some battings require prewashing or other prepara-tion before being layered into the quilt. Purchase a batting size at least 4" longer and 4" wider than your finished quilt top.

LAYERING THE QUILT TOP, BATTING, AND BACKING

Measure the width and length of the quilt top through the center. Cut and assemble the backing so it extends at least 2" beyond the quilt top on all four sides. Press seam allowances open. Note: All quilt backings in this book have vertical seams unless oth-erwise noted.

Lay the backing fabric on a smooth, flat surface, wrong side up. Pull the edges of the backing taut. Tape or pin at corners and intervals along the edge to maintain tautness. Keep edges as straight as pos-sible and corners square. Spread the batting over the backing and trim the batting to match. Center the quilt top on the batting and backing. Starting at the center of the quilt, pin all three layers together with 1" safety pins. Working out from the center, pin about every 8".

After the quilt has been basted, release the tape or pins at the edge of the backing, fold the backing over the batting, and pin to seal the edges.

Begin quilting in the center of the quilt. Continue to enlarge the quilted area from the center out.

BINDING THE QUILT
CALCULATING FABRIC REQUIREMENTS

For a smooth, durable finish, cut binding strips on the bias, fold the strips in half lengthwise, and bind your quilt with this doubled strip. To obtain a long, continuous bias strip, use the following speed-cutting technique that starts with a square of fabric. Use a calculator to determine the size of the square needed by following these simple steps:

1. Find the distance, in inches, around the quilt: two lengths plus two widths.
2. Add 10" for overlapping the ends and mitering the corners.
3. Multiply this number by the width of the binding you plan to cut.
4. Push the square-root symbol on the calculator.
5. Round the answer to the next highest whole number.
6. Add the width of the binding you plan to cut.

Example
(85" x 100" quilt)

1. (2 x 85") + (2 x 100") = 370"
2. 370" + 10" = 380"
3. 380" x 2"-wide binding = 760
4. square root of 760 = 27.568
5. 27.568 rounds up to 28
6. 28 + 2"-wide binding = 30" square

MAKING BIAS BINDING

Cut a square of binding fabric the size determined. Cut it in half diagonally. Place the two triangles together with right sides facing and edges even. Stitch by machine, leaving a ¼" seam allowance. Press open.

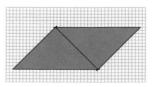

You can use the grid on a rotary cutting mat for guidelines. Place the piece, wrong side down, with bias edges parallel to the long lines of the mat.

butting
line

Fold the upper tip down to meet the seam line. Fold the lower tip up to meet the seam line so that the straight of grain edges meet on the diagonal. Do not overlap the edges. This diagonal is the butting line. Secure with pins.

Keep the bias edges even on the left side and as even as possible on the right. (If you are left handed, reverse these directions.) Begin cutting the binding to the desired width from the left. Stop cutting about 1" before the butting line and start again 1" after it. The cut should not cross the butting line. Continue to cut across the fabric in parallel lines, interrupting each cut at the butting line.

discard
last
strip

Lift up the end of strip A and use scissors to complete the cut at the butting line. Repeat for the last strip H. To realign the strips in the next step, draw ¼" seam lines on both ends at the butting line. Then mark where each cut will cross the drawn seam lines you have just drawn, by finger creasing a fold from each cut to the butting line.

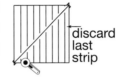

Realign the fabric edges at the butting line by moving the bottom strips to the right one strip. Pin the edges right sides together, using the folds and drawn seam lines as guides. The seam will not lie flat. Stitch on the drawn seam lines to form a tube. Press the seam allowances open. Cut across the previously uncut portions of fabric. The result is a long, continuous strip.

ATTACHING BINDING WITH MITERED CORNERS

Starting about 12" from a corner, align the raw edges of the binding with the raw edge of the quilt top. (Leave about 8" of the beginning of the strip unsewn so you can finish the ends later.) Stitch the binding to the quilt with a ¼" seam allowance. At the corners, stop stitch-

ing at the seam line for the next side of the quilt. Backstitch to secure the seam. Fold the binding to the back of the quilt and finger crease at the fold. Fold the binding up at a 45° angle at the corner. Then fold down and align the creased fold with the top edge of the quilt and the raw binding edge with the quilt edge. Begin sewing where the previous stitching stopped; back stitch to secure.

Continue sewing the binding strip to the quilt edges, repeating the mitering steps at each corner. Stop stitching about 8" from the point where you began sewing.

JOINING BINDING ENDS

Insert a straight pin in the quilt, in the center between the beginning and ending of the stitching lines. Smooth the binding in place and pin the strips to each other, but not to the quilt at the point where the center pin is inserted. Remove the first pin.

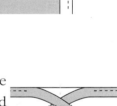

Measuring from the remaining pin, trim off the ends of the bind-ing strips, leaving a tail on each that is the width of the folded binding.

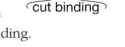

cut binding

To join the strips at a 45° angle, remove the pin and open the left strip, wrong side up. Open the right strip, right side up.

A B

Place end A on top of end B, right sides together and stitch diagonally from inside corner to inside corner.

stop at seam line

quilt top

fold

quilt top

45° angle

quilt top

fold

quilt top

quilt top

Trim off the excess fabric, leaving a ¼" seam allowance.

Finger press the seam allowance open. Refold the strip and finish sewing the binding to the quilt.

FINISHING THE BINDING

Fold the binding over the raw edges of the quilt. Using thread to match the binding, blind stitch the binding to the back of the quilt. Be careful not to let the stitches come through to the other side.

At the corners, fold the binding to create a miter, and stitch the miter closed. You may also want to secure the mitered corners with a few stitches on the front and back.

FRENCH BINDING

This technique requires a separate binding strip for each side of the quilt. To determine the length of each strip, measure each side of your quilt and add about 1" at each end for ease in finishing the corners. Cut straight or bias strips 2¾" wide by the lengths determined. Fold the strips in half lengthwise, wrong sides together, and press. Place the raw edges of the binding on the trimmed edge of the quilt top. Sew with a ¼" seam allowance. Repeat for the opposite side of the quilt.

Pull all of the binding to the back of the quilt. Press to keep the edges smooth. Sew the binding in place.

Sew binding strips to the remaining two sides of the quilt, overlapping the binding already sewn in place. Pull all the binding completely to the back again.

Trim away any bulk in the corners. Fold in the ends even with the quilt edge and stitch the binding in place.

SIGNING YOUR QUILT

Signing a quilt can be as simple as writing your name with a permanent-ink fabric pen or as involved as an embroidered cross-stitch project.

Include on your label, or on the quilt itself, your name as the quiltmaker (add your maiden name), the date the quilt was finished, and city and state. Use the label to tell the story of the quilt. Give as much information as possible.

Iron a square of muslin on a piece of freezer paper for ease in writing and, using a permanent fine-point pen, write slowly. Remove the freezer paper and press under a ¼" allowance on the top and one adjoining side of the label. Position the label on the quilt back so that the two unturned sides will be caught in the seam when the binding is attached. Hand stitch the folded edges to the quilt backing.

ATTACHING A SLEEVE

Cut a 9"-wide strip the width of the quilt, less 2". On each end, turn under ¼", then turn under another ¼" and stitch to hem both ends. Fold the fabric in half lengthwise, wrong sides together. Align the raw edges of the sleeve with the top edge of the quilt before attaching the binding. When the binding is attached, the sleeve seam will be included in the binding seam. Baste the lower edge of the sleeve through the backing and batting, taking a stitch through to the front of the quilt about every 1½". If matching thread or a neutral color is used, the stitches on the front will not be visible.

A hanging sleeve can also be added to a finished/ bound quilt. After hemming both ends of the strip, fold the fabric in half lengthwise with wrong sides together and stitch a ¼" seam, forming a tube. Press the seam allowance open and center the seam on the back of the tube. Press. Align the sleeve ½" below the binding along the top of the quilt. Baste the sleeve to the quilt through the backing and batting, taking a stitch through to the front of the quilt about every 1½".

SETTING BLOCKS ON POINT
Diagonal Measurement

SIZE OF BLOCK	DECIMAL	NEAREST FRACTION
1	1.414	1½
1½	2.121	2⅛
2	2.828	2⅞
2	3.535	3⅝
3	4.242	4¼
3½	4.949	5
4	5.656	5⅝
4½	6.363	6⅜
5	7.070	7⅛
5½	7.777	7⅞
6	8.484	8½
6½	9.191	9¼
7	9.898	10
7½	10.605	10⅝
8	11.312	11⅜
8½	12.019	12⅛
9	12.726	12¾
9½	13.433	12½
10	14.140	14¼
10½	14.847	14⅞
11	15.554	15⅝
11½	16.261	16⅜
12	16.968	17
12½	17.675	17¾
13	18.382	18½
13½	19.089	19⅛
14	19.796	19⅞
14½	20.503	20½
15	21.210	21¼
15½	21.917	22
16	22.624	22⅝

(All measurements are in inches.)

SIDE AND CORNER TRIANGLES

Finished Block Size	Square Size to Cut for Corner Triangles ▢		Square Size to Cut for Side Triangles ⊠	
	DECIMAL	NEAREST FRACTION	DECIMAL	NEAREST FRACTION
1	1.582	1⅝	2.664	2¾
1½	1.935	2	3.371	3⅜
2	2.289	2⅜	4.078	4⅛
2½	2.75	2¾	4.785	4⅞
3	2.996	3	5.492	5½
3½	3.349	3⅝	6.199	6¼
4	3.703	3¾	6.906	7
4½	4.056	4⅛	7.613	7⅝
5	4.410	4½	8.320	8⅜
5½	4.763	4⅞	9.027	9⅛
6	5.117	5⅛	9.734	9¾
6½	5.471	5½	10.441	10½
7	5.824	5⅞	11.148	11¼
7½	6.200	6¼	11.900	12
8	6.531	6⅝	12.571	12⅝
8½	6.884	6⅞	13.269	13⅜
9	7.238	7¼	13.976	14
9½	7.592	7⅝	14.683	14¾
10	7.945	8	15.390	15½
10½	8.299	8⅜	16.097	16⅛
11	8.75	8¾	16.804	16⅞
11½	9.006	9⅛	17.5	17½
12	9.359	9⅜	18.218	18¼
12½	9.713	9¾	18.925	19
13	10.066	10⅛	19.632	19¾
13½	10.420	10½	20.339	20⅜
14	10.773	10⅞	21.046	21⅛
14½	11.127	11⅛	21.753	21¾
15	11.480	11½	22.460	22½
15½	11.834	11⅞	23.167	23¼
16	12.187	12¼	23.874	23⅞

(All measurements are in inches.)

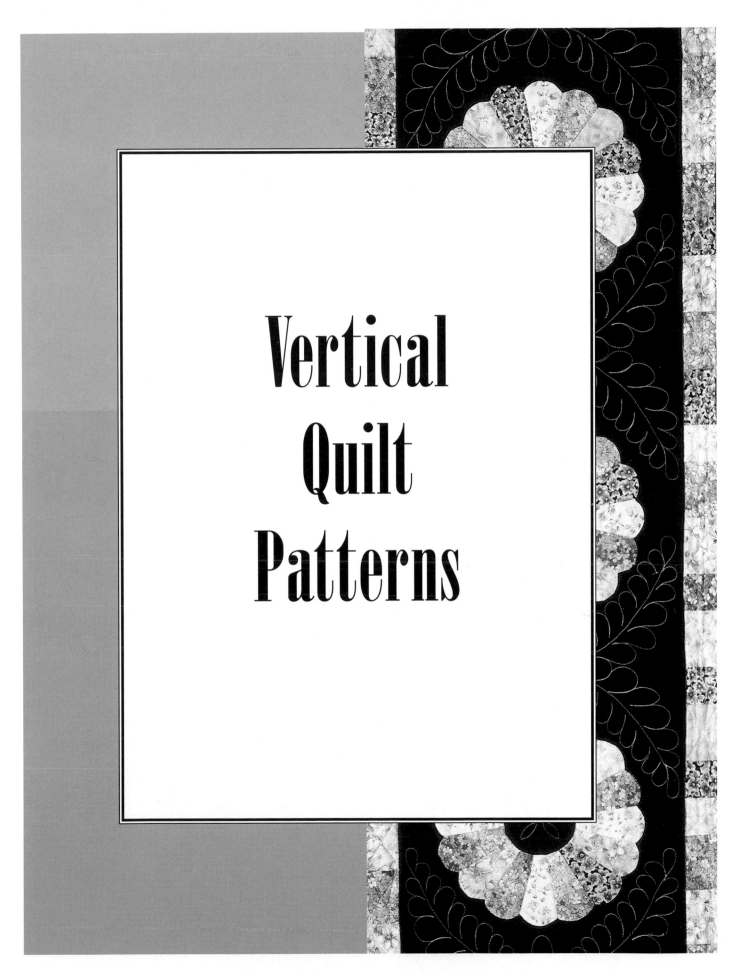

Vertical Quilt Patterns

MORE VERTICAL QUILTS WITH STYLE – BOBBIE A. AUG & SHARON NEWMAN

Using Squares

Four and Nine

Quilt size 59½" x 85"
Block size 6" x 6"

FABRIC REQUIREMENTS

FOUR AND NINE PATCHES:

Scraps of about 25 fabrics. (If you want to strip piece the patches, fat eighths or fat quarters may be used.)

BACKGROUND:

8 to 10 fat quarters of assorted prints

SASHING, BORDERS, AND BINDING:

4 yards of print

BACKING:

5¼ yards

CUTTING LIST
(for strip piecing)

NINE-PATCH PRINTS:

8 dark strips 2½" x 21"

7 light and medium strips 2½" x 21"

FOUR-PATCH PRINTS:

6 dark strips 3½" x 21"

6 light and medium strips 3½" x 21"

BACKGROUND PRINTS:

11 squares 9¾" x 9¾", cut twice diagonally, for side triangles (two will be extra)

14 squares 5⅛" x 5⅛", cut once diagonally, for corner triangles

BORDER AND SASHING PRINT:

4 strips 9" x 68½" for sashing and side borders

2 strips 9" x 43" for top and bottom borders

FOUR AND NINE (59" x 84"), MADE BY BOBBIE AUG.
This quilt is a perfect example of how beautiful simplicity can be. Two simple blocks combined with a wonderful print is all that is required for a successful quilt.

Four and Nine

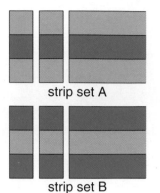

strip set A

strip set B

FIGURE 1. Cut 2½" segments.

A   B   A   Make 12

FIGURE 2. Assemble Nine-Patch blocks.

SEWING DIRECTIONS

Make 12 Nine-Patch blocks (2½" squares) and 16 Four-Patch blocks (3½" squares) by cutting individual patches or strip piecing as follows:

PIECING THE NINE PATCHES

✦ Using two contrasting fabrics, make three strip sets with dark strips on the outside and a light strip in the center (strip set A).

✦ Using the same contrasting fabrics, sew two strip sets with light strips on the outside and a dark strip in the center (strip set B).

✦ Cut 2½" segments from each set (Figure 1).

✦ Assemble the Nine Patches from two segments of strip set A and one segment of strip set B to make 12 Nine Patches (Figure 2).

PIECING THE FOUR PATCHES

✦ Using one dark and one light or medium strip, sew a lengthwise seam. Press the seam allowances to the darker print. Make six strip sets.

✦ Cut 3½" segments from the joined strips and sew two together to make 16 Four Patches.

PIECING THE PANELS

✦ Arrange three columns of Four and Nine Patches set on point. Alternate blocks beginning with a Nine-Patch block on columns 1 and 3. Begin the center column with a Four Patch block. Each column consists of eight blocks of 4 Four Patches and 4 Nine Patches.

✦ For each of the three columns, add corner triangles and side triangles as shown (Figure 3).

ASSEMBLING THE QUILT TOP

✦ Mark the sashing strips and the side borders with a ¼" seam allowance at each end and at 8½" intervals.

✦ Refer to the photograph on page 15 and arrange the columns, sashing strips, and side borders. Pin and sew the strips, matching the points with the seams. Press.

✦ Make four corner blocks by adding corner triangles to the Four-Patch blocks (Figure 4).

✦ Sew the corner blocks to each end of the top and bottom border strips.

✦ Join the top and bottom borders to the quilt top. Press.

FINISHING THE QUILT

✦ Mark a quilting design. The Four and Nine Patches are quilted in the ditch on this quilt. The setting triangles are quilted in a continuous triangle design. A leaf pattern from the floral print was used in the sashing and borders.

✦ Layer the quilt top, batting, and backing. Baste and quilt.

✦ Bind, sign, and date your quilt.

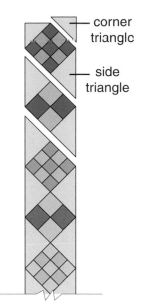
corner triangle

side triangle

FIGURE 3. Make two columns beginning with a Nine-Patch block and one column beginning with a Four-Patch block.

corner triangle

FIGURE 4. Assemble four corner blocks.

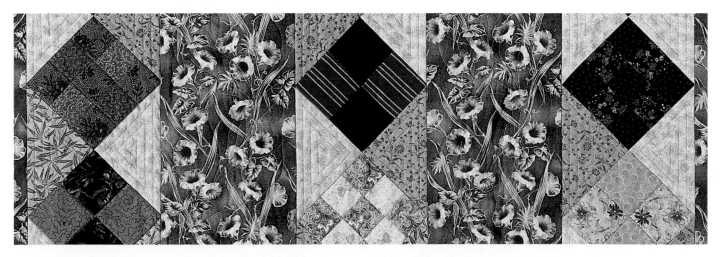

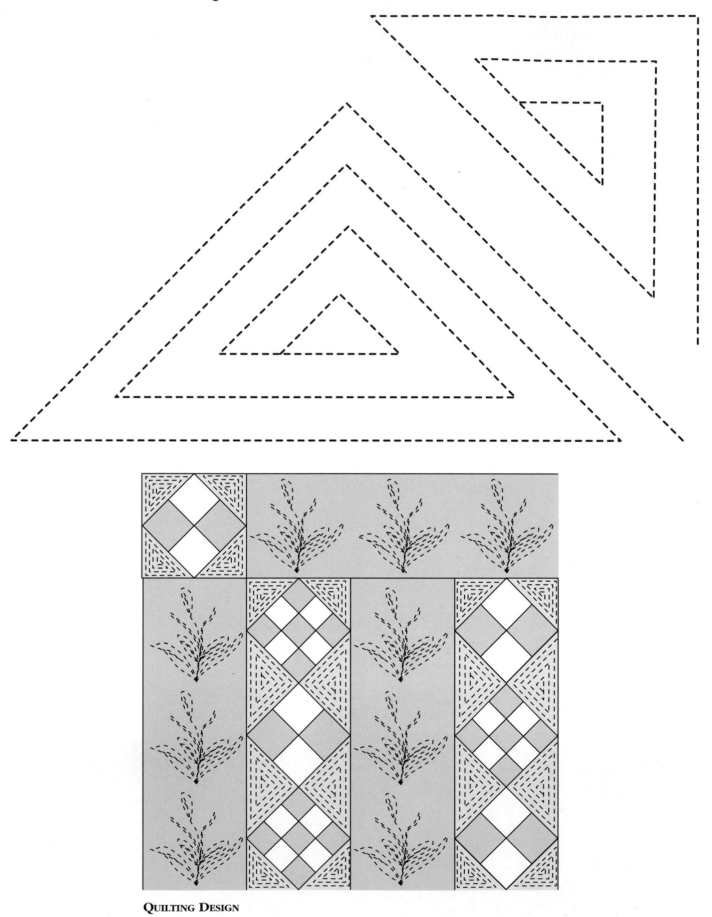

QUILTING DESIGN

More Vertical Quilts with Style — Bobbie A. Aug & Sharon Newman

One and Four-Vermont

Quilt size 73" x 81½"
Block size 3½" x 3½"

You can make your quilt from scraps, or use the following directions for a strip-pieced quilt made from two striped fabrics. Other types of fabrics would be charming, too.

FABRIC REQUIREMENTS

STRIPE I:
2⅛ yards

STRIPE II:
2⅛ yards

PATCHWORK:
½ yard light prints
¾ yard dark prints
¾ yard solid white

BACKGROUND:
1¾ yards of medium and dark prints

BORDERS AND BINDING:
2¼ yards

BACKING:
5 yards

CUTTING LIST

STRIPE I:
4 strips 6" x 70½" for sashing

STRIPE II:
2 strips 6" x 70½" for sashing
2 strips 3" x 70½" for side borders

(Cutting List continued on page 22)

ONE AND FOUR – VERMONT (76" x 84"), MAKER UNKNOWN, C. 1880. This quilt is from Sharon's collection. It is a typical scrap bar quilt from the Northeast, showcasing the brown-striped fabrics.

One and Four–Vermont

(Cutting List continued)

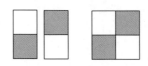

FIGURE 1. Cut 2¼" segments.

FIGURE 2. Assemble Four-Patch blocks.

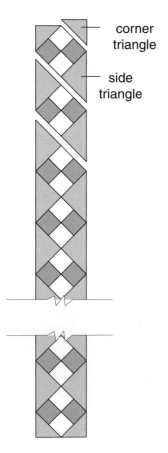

corner triangle

side triangle

FIGURE 3. Make five columns of 14 Four-Patches and two columns of 14 light-print squares.

LIGHT PRINTS:

28 squares 4" x 4"

DARK PRINTS:

9 strips 2¼" x 40"

SOLID WHITE:

9 strips 2¼" x 40"

BACKGROUND:

14 squares 3⅜" x 3⅜", cut once diagonally, for corner triangles

 46 squares 6¼" x 6¼", cut twice diagonally, for side triangles

TOP AND BOTTOM BORDERS:

2 strips 6½" x 73½"

SEWING DIRECTIONS

PIECING THE BLOCKS

✦ Sew the dark print and solid white strips in pairs. Cut 140 segments 2¼" wide from the pieced strips (Figure 1).

✦ Sew two of the segments together to make a Four-Patch block (Figure 2). Make 70 Four Patches.

PIECING THE PANELS

✦ Arrange two columns of 14 light-print squares, set on point.

✦ Arrange five columns of 14 Four-Patch blocks, set on point.

✦ For each of the seven columns, add corner triangles and side triangles as shown (Figure 3).

ASSEMBLING THE QUILT TOP

✦ Mark the sashing strips ¼" from the edge at each corner and at 5" intervals.

✦ Arrange the columns and stripes, placing the columns with light-print squares on the outside edges. Arrange the two stripes in mirror-image fashion. Pin and sew the pieced columns and sashing strips, matching the marked points with seams. Press.

✦ Sew the side borders to the quilt top.

✦ Add the top and bottom borders to complete the quilt top. Press.

FINISHING THE QUILT

✦ Mark a quilting design. This quilt is sparsely quilted with diagonal lines 5" apart over the stripes, a vertical line through the center of the Four Patches and squares, and horizontal lines through the squares and Four Patches.

✦ Layer the quilt top, batting, and backing. Baste.

✦ Quilt and bind.

✦ Sign and date your quilt.

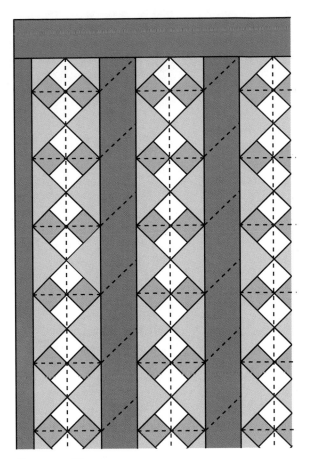

QUILTING DESIGN

More Vertical Quilts with Style – Bobbie A. Aug & Sharon Newman

Using Rectangles
Primary Colors

Quilt size 41" x 58"
Block size 3" x 3"

FABRIC REQUIREMENTS

BACKGROUND:

1 yard white

COLOR STRIPS:

1½ yards red
1½ yards yellow
1½ yards blue

SASHING AND BORDERS:

1½ yards print

BACKING:

3 yards (seam horizontally)

BINDING:

½ yard

CUTTING LIST

WHITE:

6 strips 1½" x 17"
6 strips 2½" x 17"

 15 squares 5½" x 5½", cut twice diagonally, for side triangles

6 squares 3" x 3", cut once diagonally, for corner triangles

COLOR STRIPS:

2 strips 1½" x 47" of each color for sashing
3 strips 1½" x 17" of each color

PRINT:

4 strips 6" x 47" for sashing and side borders
2 strips 6" x 42½" for top and bottom borders

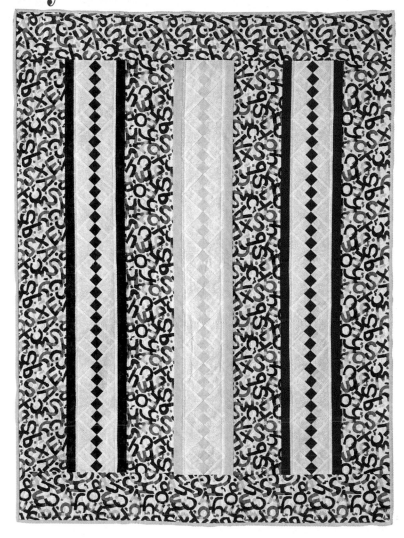

PRIMARY COLORS (42½" x 58"), MADE BY BARBARA F. SHIE, COLORADO SPRINGS, COLORADO. The rotary-cutting, machine-piecing method for sewing Seminole Patchwork is a great way to quickly sew a crib quilt for a perfect shower gift.

Primary Colors

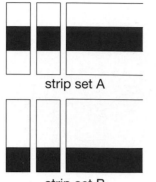

strip set A

strip set B

FIGURE 1. Cut 1½" segments.

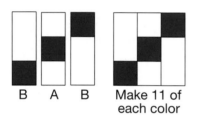

B   A   B   Make 11 of each color

FIGURE 2. Assemble color blocks.

corner triangle

side triangle

FIGURE 3. Make three columns of 11 blocks.

SEWING DIRECTIONS

PIECING THE BLOCKS

✦ Sew 1½" x 17" white strips to each side of a 1½" x 17" red (strip set A). Repeat for blue and yellow. Press the seam allowances toward the dark strips.

✦ Sew a 2½" x 17" white strip to a 1½" x 17" red (strip set B). Repeat for blue and yellow. Make two of each color. Press the seam allowances toward the dark strips.

✦ Cut eleven 1½" segments from each pieced strip (Figure 1).

✦ Sew the segments into blocks of the same color (Figure 2). Make 11 blocks of each color.

PIECING THE COLUMNS

✦ Arrange one column of each color including blocks, side tri-angles, and corner triangles as shown (Figure 3).

✦ Mark the 1½" x 47" sashing strips and columns at the half and quarter points. Sew the sashing strips to the columns.

ASSEMBLING THE QUILT TOP

✦ Add the print sashing, starting and ending with a sashing strip.

✦ Sew the top and bottom borders to the quilt top.

FINISHING THE QUILT

✦ Mark a quilting design. This quilt is machine stitched in outlines of the vertical sashing strips with a large-scale stippling design over the border.

✦ Layer the quilt top, batting, and backing. Baste.

✦ Quilt and bind.

✦ Sign and date your quilt.

QUILTING DESIGN

Blocks and Bars

Quilt size 75" x 78"
Block size 10" x 10"

FABRIC REQUIREMENTS

SASHING AND BORDERS:
2¼ yards solid maroon

BLOCK CENTER:
⅝ yard red plaid

PIECED BARS AND BLOCKS:
Plaids, stripes, chambrays, and solids to total
2¼ yards

BACKING:
4⅞ yards

BINDING:
¾ yard

CUTTING LIST

MAROON:
6 strips 2¾" x 73" for sashing
2 strips 3¼" x 69¾" for top and bottom
     borders
2 strips 3¼" x 78½" for side borders
20 strips 3" x 10½"

RED PLAID:
24 strips 3½" x 10½"

PLAIDS, STRIPES, CHAMBRAYS, AND SOLIDS:
Strips in 1", 1½", 1¾", 2", and 2¼" widths, cut
     into 4" and 5¾" lengths

SEWING DIRECTIONS

PIECING THE BARS

✦ Sew 5¾" pieces in random order of color and size to equal 73" long. Make three columns of bars.

✦ Join a maroon sashing strip to each side of the three bars.

PIECING THE BLOCKS

✦ Sew 4" strips in random order of color and size to equal 10½" long. Make 48 pieced strips.

✦ Sew a red plaid strip between two pieced strips to make a block (Figure 1). Make 24 blocks.

ASSEMBLING THE QUILT TOP

✦ Refer to the photograph and join six blocks with maroon sashing strips. Make four columns.

✦ Combine the block rows with the bar units, starting with a block row.

✦ Add the border strips to the top and bottom of the quilt. Add the side borders to complete the quilt top.

FINISHING THE QUILT

✦ Mark a quilting design. Straight lines have been quilted through the center of each sashing and border in this quilt. The sashes and all pieces have been quilted "by the piece," which means ¼" from all the seams.

✦ Layer the quilt top, batting, and backing. Baste.

✦ Quilt and bind.

✦ Sign and date your quilt.

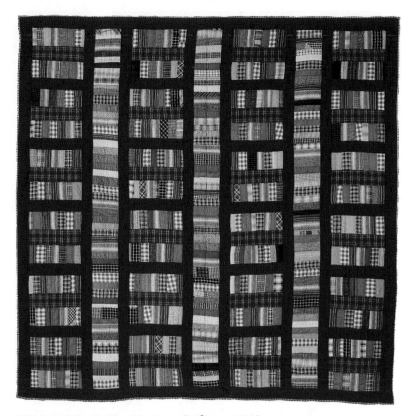

BLOCKS AND BARS (76" x 78"), MAKER UNKNOWN. This quilt is from Sharon's collection and was made during the first quarter of the twentieth century. The use of several plaids, stripes, and chambrays is typical of many quilts made during this era. The backing is a printed black and white check.

FIGURE 1. Make 24 blocks.

QUILTING DESIGN

MORE VERTICAL QUILTS WITH STYLE – BOBBIE A. AUG & SHARON NEWMAN

Using Triangles
Triangles and Bars

Quilt Size 44½" x 53"

FABRIC REQUIREMENTS

RED TRIANGLES AND BINDING:

½ yard print

BLUE TRIANGLES, SASHING, AND BORDERS:

2¼ yards prints

WHITE TRIANGLES:

1⅛ yards print

BACKING:

2⅞ yards (seam horizontally)

CUTTING LIST

RED PRINT:

9 squares 3⅜" x 3⅜", cut once diagonally

BLUE PRINTS:

97 squares 3⅜" x 3⅜", cut once diagonally

11 strips 2" x 46½" for sashing
2 strips 2" x 49½" for side borders
2 strips 2" x 38¼" for top and bottom borders

WHITE PRINT:

110 squares 3⅜" x 3⅜", cut once diagonally

TRIANGLES AND BARS (31" x 36"), MADE BY SHARON NEWMAN AND MACHINE QUILTED BY SARA VOYLES, LUBBOCK, TEXAS. Inspired by a crib quilt made in Massachusetts, c. 1860, the reduced scale and pattern variation on this quilt are typical of early crib quilts that were based on full-size patterns.

Triangles and Bars

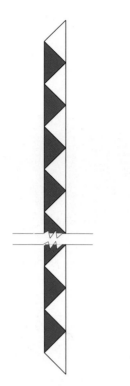

FIGURE 1. Sew along the short sides of the white and blue triangles to make 12 strips.

SEWING DIRECTIONS

PIECING THE TRIANGLES

✦ Sew 14 white triangles and 13 blue triangles together along the short sides as shown (Figure 1), starting with white and alternating colors. Randomly substitute 10 red triangles for blue triangles. Make 12 pieced strips.

✦ For the outer borders, piece two strips, starting and ending with red triangles. Use 14 white triangles and 13 blue triangles for each side border strip.

✦ For the top and bottom borders, piece two strips, starting and ending with red triangles. Use 12 white triangles and 11 blue triangles for the border strips.

ASSEMBLING THE QUILT TOP

✦ Sew a blue sashing strip between two pieced strips, placing the long sides of the blue triangles against the sashing. Set the top edge of the sashing ¼" above the point of the blue triangle. Make six sets. Trim the white triangles even with the top of the sashing strips, leaving ¼" for seam allowances (Figure 2).

✦ Sew blue sashing strips between the sets.

✦ Add blue border strips at the top and bottom of the quilt top.

✦ Add blue border strips at the sides of the quilt top.

¼"

¼"

FIGURE 2. Trim the white triangles even with the top and bottom of the strips.

✦ Add pieced borders at the sides, top, and bottom of the quilt top. Miter the corners, joining the red triangles (Figure 3). Trim to ¼" seam allowances.

FINISHING THE QUILT

✦ Mark a quilting design. Alternate blue strips in this quilt are quilted with a double-line cable. The outer border is quilted in ovals of two sizes.

✦ Layer the quilt top, batting, and backing. Baste.

✦ Quilt and bind.

✦ Sign and date your quilt.

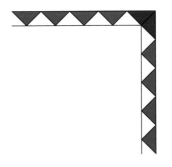

FIGURE 3. Miter the corners using red triangles.

QUILTING DESIGN

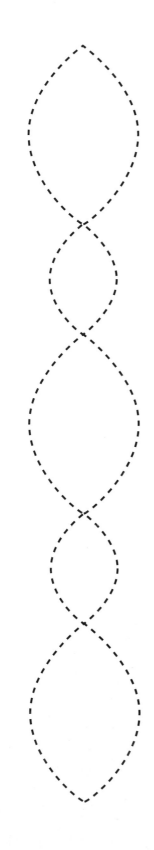

Pink and Yellow Zigzag

Quilt size 63½" x 63½"

When choosing fabrics for your quilt, note the contrast between the two fabrics. If there is low contrast, the zigzags will be subtle. If the fabrics have high contrast, the zigzags will produce a striking lightning-bolt effect.

FABRIC REQUIREMENTS

BORDERS AND BINDING:

2 yards blue

TRIANGLES:

2⅓ yards pink
2⅓ yards yellow

BACKING:

4 yards light color

CUTTING LIST

PINK TRIANGLES:

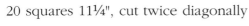 20 squares 11¼", cut twice diagonally

YELLOW TRIANGLES:

20 squares 11¼", cut twice diagonally

BLUE BORDER:

4 strips 2¼" x 65½"

PINK AND YELLOW ZIGZAG (63" x 63"), MAKER UNKNOWN, QUILTED BY BOBBIE AUG AND DEBRA ANDREW, AURORA, COLORADO. Bobbie purchased this crib-size quilt top from an antique quilt dealer at the American Quilter's Society Show and Contest in Paducah, Kentucky. The borders were "wobbly" and needed repair. Rather than disturb the original stitching, after it was quilted, Bobbie folded the border back on itself to visually cut the size in half and form a binding.

Pink and Yellow Zigzag

FIGURE 1. Sew 13 triangles for each column.

strip 1   strip 2

FIGURE 2. Match the triangle center and points to join columns.

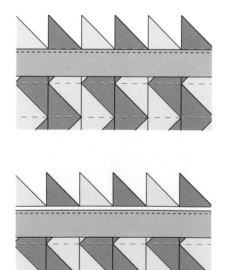

FIGURE 3. Sew the border to the quilt and trim excess triangle pieces from behind the border.

SEWING DIRECTIONS

PIECING THE COLUMNS

✦ Alternating between pink and yellow, arrange the triangles into six columns of 13 triangles, beginning and ending with a yellow triangle. Sew the triangles together with the longest side of each triangle toward the outside of the columns. Make another six columns that begin and end with pink triangles (Figure 1). Press.

ASSEMBLING THE QUILT TOP

✦ Mark the centers of the long sides of the triangles. Arrange the columns as shown in the photo on page 35, alternating colors. Pin the columns together, matching the triangle centers to the triangle points in adjacent columns to create a zigzag effect (Figure 2). Note: The top and bottom edges will be irregularly shaped. Press.

ADDING THE BORDERS

✦ Add the side borders to the quilt top. Press.

✦ Pin the top and bottom borders to the quilt where the two triangles come together. Using a ¼" seam allowance, sew the borders to the quilt with mitered corners. Press. Trim off the triangle extensions (Figure 3).

FINISHING THE QUILT

✦ Mark a quilting design. The design chosen for this quilt is ¼" echo quilting inside each triangle. The border was quilted in two parallel straight lines.

✦ Layer the quilt top, batting, and backing. Baste.

✦ Quilt and bind.

✦ Sign and date your quilt.

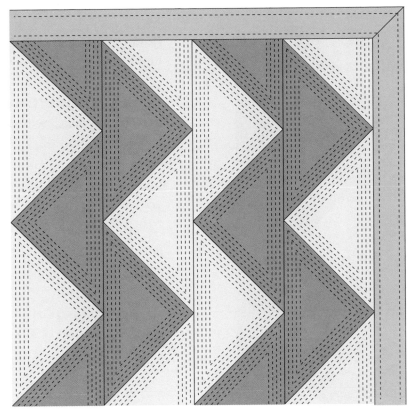

QUILTING DESIGN

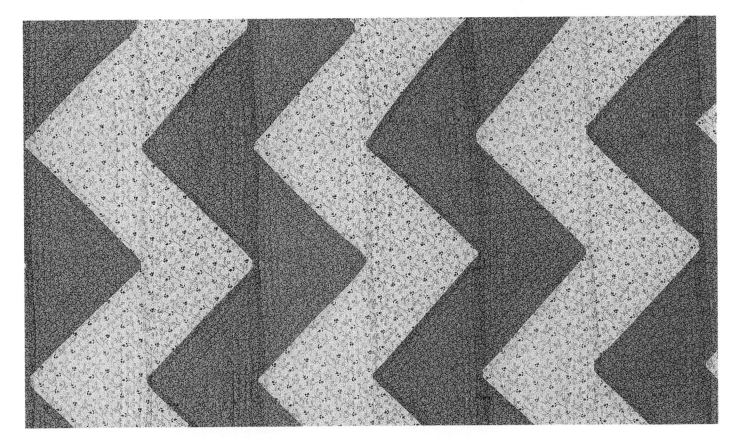

Hourglass

Quilt size 41½" x 55"
Block size 4¾" x 4¾"

FABRIC REQUIREMENTS

BLOCKS, BORDERS, SASHING, AND BINDING:
2 yards dark batik

SASHING AND BLOCKS:
1½ yards light batik

BACKING:
2¾ yards (seam horizontally)

CUTTING LIST

DARK:

3 strips 5" x 43¼" for side borders and middle sashing

2 strips 6½" x 42" for top and bottom borders

⊠ 18 squares 6" x 6", cut twice diagonally

LIGHT:

2 strips 5" x 43¼" for sashing

⊠ 18 squares 6" x 6", cut twice diagonally

SEWING DIRECTIONS

PIECING THE PANELS

✦ Sew triangles of light and dark in pairs as shown. Make 72 units.

✦ Join the two pieced units to complete the block. Make 36 blocks.

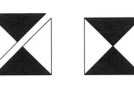

✦ Join nine blocks in four strips, alternating the direction of the blocks as shown in the photograph.

ASSEMBLING THE QUILT TOP

✦ Mark the pieced columns and strips at half and quarter intervals.

✦ Arrange the pieced columns and sashing as shown in the photograph, beginning and ending with pieced columns. Press.

✦ Sew the side borders to the quilt top. Add the top and bottom borders to complete the quilt top.

FINISHING THE QUILT

✦ Mark a quilting design. Diagonal lines are machine quilted in HOURGLASS, outlining the blocks and extending over sashing and borders.

✦ Layer the quilt top, batting, and backing. Baste.

✦ Quilt and bind.

✦ Sign and date your quilt.

HOURGLASS (41" x 53"), MADE BY BARBARA F. SHIE, COLORADO SPRINGS, COLORADO. This is a two-fabric quilt that utilizes contrast to execute the design. The blocks display Barbara's favorite color beautifully.

QUILTING DESIGN

MORE VERTICAL QUILTS WITH STYLE – BOBBIE A. AUG & SHARON NEWMAN

Pastel Pinwheels

Quilt size 44½" x 54"
Block size 5" x 5"

FABRIC REQUIREMENTS

BACKGROUND:

1⅝ yards light

PINWHEELS:

6 fat quarters of different prints

BORDERS AND BINDING:

1½ yards prints

BACKING:

2⅞ yards (seam horizontally)

CUTTING LIST

BACKGROUND:

64 squares 3⅜" x 3⅜"

5 strips 4" x 40½" for inner side borders

2 strips 4" x 38" for inner top and bottom borders

PRINTS:

11 squares 3⅜" x 3⅜" of each

BORDERS:

2 strips 4" x 47½" for outer side borders

2 strips 4" x 45" for outer top and bottom borders

PASTEL PINWHEELS (45" x 54"), MADE BY BARBARA F. SHIE, COLORADO SPRINGS, COLORADO. Barbara is a prolific quiltmaker, choosing the sewing machine for her piecing. She used pastel fabric scraps left over from an earlier project to make this sweet baby quilt.

Pastel Pinwheels

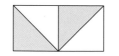

FIGURE 1. Make 128 half-square units.

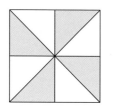

FIGURE 2. Join the half-square units to make 64 units.

FIGURE 3. Join the units to make 32 pinwheels.

SEWING DIRECTIONS

PIECING THE COLUMNS

✦ With right sides together, pair one background and one print square. Draw a diagonal line on the background square. Sew ¼" from the line on both sides of the line. Cut on the line and press the seam allowances toward the dark triangle to make the two half-square units. Make 128 units (Figure 1).

✦ Join the half-square units in pairs (Figure 2). Make 64 units.

✦ Join the pairs to create pinwheels (Figure 3). Make 32 pinwheels.

✦ Sew four strips of eight pinwheels each, arranging the colors in random order.

MORE VERTICAL QUILTS WITH STYLE – BOBBIE A. AUG & SHARON NEWMAN

ASSEMBLING THE QUILT TOP

✦ Mark the pieced panels and sashing strips at half and quarter points.

✦ Arrange the panels and sashing strips, beginning and ending with sashing strips. Press.

✦ Sew the background border strips to the top and bottom of the quilt top.

✦ Add the side, top, and bottom print borders to complete the quilt top.

FINISHING THE QUILT

✦ Mark a quilting design. This quilt is machine quilted in horizontal and vertical outlines that extend into the borders.

✦ Layer the quilt top, batting, and backing. Baste.

✦ Quilt and bind.

✦ Sign and date your quilt.

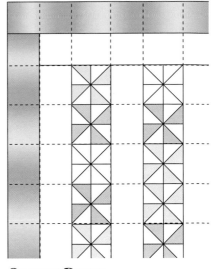

QUILTING DESIGN

MORE VERTICAL QUILTS WITH STYLE – BOBBIE A. AUG & SHARON NEWMAN

Sawtooth Stars

Quilt size 86" x 99"
Block size 6" x 6"

FABRIC REQUIREMENTS

SASHING, BORDERS, AND BINDING:

5¼ yards green print

BACKGROUND AND SASHING:

4¼ yards cream

STAR PRINTS:

39 fat eighths

BACKING:

8¼ yards

CUTTING LIST

GREEN PRINT:

8 strips 2½" x 93⅞", cut lengthwise, for sashing and side borders

2 strips 2½" x 86½", cut lengthwise, for top
and bottom borders

14 squares 5⅛" x 5⅛", cut once
diagonally, for corner triangles

35 squares 9¾" x 9¾", cut twice
diagonally, for side triangles

CREAM:

14 strips 1¼" x 93⅞", cut lengthwise, for sashing and side borders

2 strips 1¼" x 86½", cut lengthwise, for top
and bottom borders

308 rectangles 2" x 3½"

308 squares 2" x 2"

STAR PRINTS:

77 center squares 3½" x 3½"

616 squares 2" x 2"

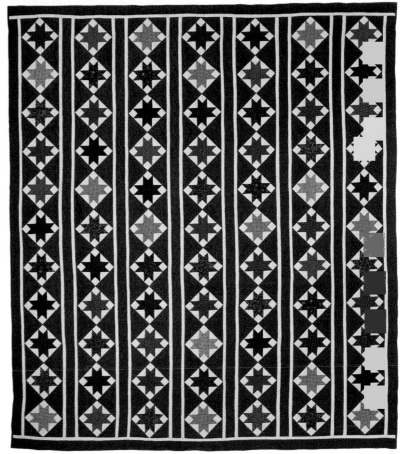

SAWTOOTH STARS (84" x 96"), MADE BY SHARON
NEWMAN AND QUILTED BY SARA VOYLES, LUBBOCK,
TEXAS. Stars have always been one of the most appealing designs
in quiltmaking. This quilt was inspired by a quilt made in 1890 in
the northeast United States.

Sawtooth Stars

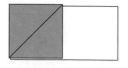

FIGURE 1. Mark a diagonal line from corner to corner.

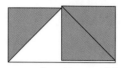

FIGURE 2. Sew on the diagonal line and trim allowing ¼" for the seam.

FIGURE 3. Sew the pieced unit with two background squares.

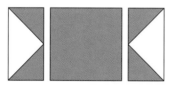

FIGURE 4. Sew the remaining pieced units to the center square.

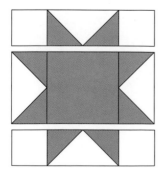

FIGURE 5. Join the units to form a star.

SEWING DIRECTIONS

PIECING THE STARS

✦ Place a print square on the end of a background rectangle with right sides together. Mark a diagonal line from corner to corner (Figure 1). Sew on the line. Trim, allowing ¼" for the seam allowances. Press.

✦ Place a second print square on the other end of the background rectangle. Sew and trim as before (Figure 2). Press. Make 308 of these units.

✦ Sew the pieced unit with a background square on each end (Figure 3). Make 154 of these units.

✦ Sew the remaining 154 pieced units on opposite sides of the center print square (Figure 4).

✦ Join the units to make 77 stars (Figure 5).

QUILTING DESIGN

PIECING THE COLUMNS

✦ Arrange seven columns of 11 Sawtooth Stars, side triangles, and corner triangles as shown (Figure 6).

ASSEMBLING THE QUILT TOP

✦ Sew the cream sashing strips on each side of the six green-print sashing strips. Sew one cream strip on each of the print border strips.

✦ Refer to the photograph on page 45 and arrange the columns, sashing strips, and side borders. Pin and sew the strips, matching the points with the seams. Press.

✦ Add the top and bottom borders.

FINISHING THE QUILT

✦ Mark a quilting design. This quilt has an oval design in the sashing strips (refer to TRIANGLES AND BARS, page 33) with curved motifs in the side and corner triangles. The stars are outline quilted.

✦ Layer the quilt top, batting, and backing. Baste.

✦ Quilt and bind.

✦ Sign and date your quilt.

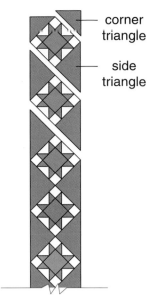

corner triangle

side triangle

FIGURE 6. Make seven columns of 11 stars.

SAWTOOTH STARS
FULL-SIZE QUILTING PATTERNS

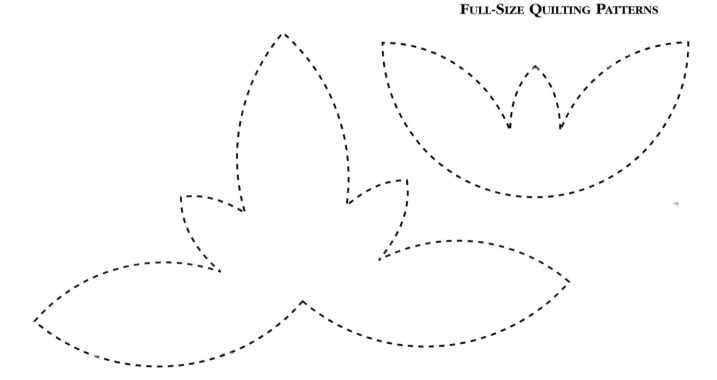

Scrap Baskets

Quilt size 58" x 68½"
Block size 8" x 8"

FABRIC REQUIREMENTS

BLOCK BACKGROUND: ⅞ yard light

BASKETS: ⅝ yard dark

FLOWERS: 3 fat eighths of different colors

SASHING AND BORDERS: 1¾ yards

SETTING TRIANGLES: 1 yard

BACKING: 3⅝ yards (seam horizontally)

BINDING: ⅔ yard

CUTTING LIST

BLOCK BACKGROUND:
30 squares 2½" x 2½"
30 rectangles 2½" x 4½"
45 squares 2⅞" x 2⅞"

BASKETS:
30 squares 2⅞" x 2⅞"
45 squares 2½" x 2½"

FLOWERS (FROM EACH OF THE THREE COLORS):
5 squares 2⅞" x 2⅞"
5 squares 2½" x 2½"

SASHING AND BORDERS:
4 strips 6½" x 57⅛" for sashing and side borders
2 strips 6½" x 58½" for top and bottom borders

SETTING TRIANGLES:

⊠ 6 squares 12⅝" x 12⅝", cut twice diagonally, for side triangles

◺ 6 squares 6⅝" x 6⅝", cut once diagonally, for corner triangles

MORE VERTICAL QUILTS WITH STYLE – BOBBIE A. AUG & SHARON NEWMAN

SEWING DIRECTIONS

PIECING THE BASKETS

✦ Place a 2⅞" square of background fabric and a 2⅞" square of flower fabric right sides together. Draw a diagonal line on the lighter fabric and sew ¼" away from the line on each side of it. Cut on the diagonal line. Press the two half-squares open. Make 30 half squares as shown (Figure 1).

✦ Place a 2⅞" square of background fabric and a 2⅞" square of basket fabric right sides together. Make 60 half-squares as described previously.

✦ Referring to the unit diagrams, use the half-squares, 2½" squares, and the rectangles to make 15 of each unit.

✦ Refer to the block assembly diagram to join units A, B, C, and D to complete the 15 blocks.

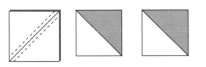

FIGURE 1. Make 30 half-square units.

SCRAP BASKETS (57" X 67"), MADE BY SHARON NEWMAN AND QUILTED BY THE CATHOLIC LADIES QUILTING GROUP, SLATON, TEXAS. Three columns of five baskets are set with a printed floral stripe. The pastel tones selected blend like flowers in a summer garden.

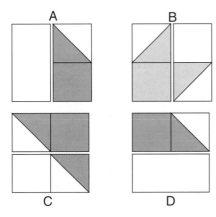

UNIT ASSEMBLY

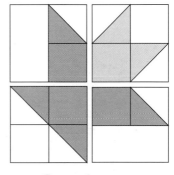

BLOCK ASSEMBLY

Scrap Baskets

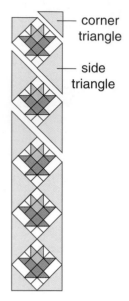

corner triangle

side triangle

FIGURE 2. Make three columns of 5 blocks.

PIECING THE COLUMNS

✦ Arrange three columns of Scrap Basket blocks, side triangles, and corner triangles, as shown (Figure 2).

ASSEMBLING THE QUILT TOP

✦ Mark the sashing strips and the side borders with a ¼" seam allowance at each end and at 11⅛" intervals.

✦ Refer to the photograph and arrange the pieced strips, sashing strips, and side borders. Pin and sew the strips, matching the marked points with the seams. Press.

✦ Join the top and bottom borders to the quilt top. Press.

FINISHING THE QUILT

✦ Mark a quilting design. The corner and side triangles on this quilt feature decorative motifs, the border and sashing are quilted in a fan design over the repeating print, and the blocks are outlined.

✦ Layer the quilt top, batting, and backing. Baste.

✦ Quilt and bind.

✦ Sign and date your quilt.

QUILTING DESIGN

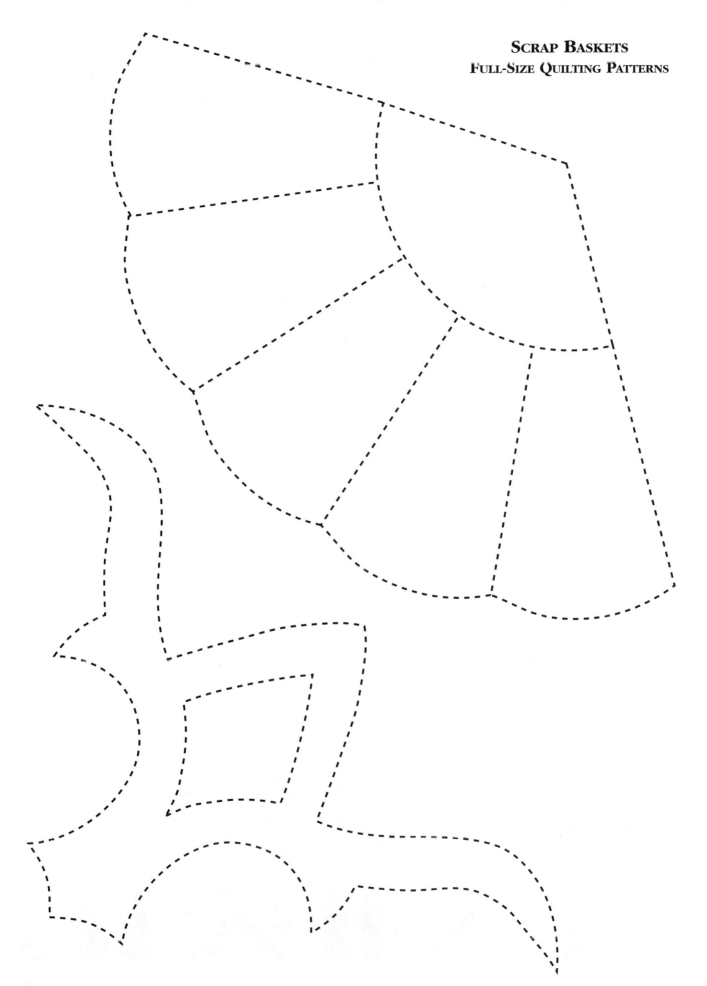

MORE VERTICAL QUILTS WITH STYLE – BOBBIE A. AUG & SHARON NEWMAN

The Lilies

Quilt size 73½" x 86½"
Lily block size 9" x 9"
Four-Patch block size 3" x 3" (sashing)

FABRIC REQUIREMENTS

BLOCKS, SASHING, BORDERS, AND BINDING:
4½ yards indigo

LILIES, SASHING, AND SETTING TRIANGLES:
4¼ yards white on white print

BACKING:
5 yards

CUTTING LIST

To avoid confusion, make all 108 small half-squares, then cut and sew one type of unit at a time.

INDIGO:

6 strips 2" x 40" for Four-Patch blocks
2 strips 5½" x 76" for top and bottom borders
2 strips 5½" x 89" for side borders
108 squares 2⅜" x 2⅜" for half-square units

24 squares 2⅜" x 2⅜", cut once diagonally, for units A and B

24 squares 5⅜" x 5⅜", cut once diagonally, for units A and B

24 squares 5⅛" x 5⅛", cut once diagonally, for unit D

24 squares 5½" x 5½", cut twice diagonally, for sashing side triangles

6 squares 3" x 3", cut once diagonally, for sashing corner triangles

6 strips 2¼" x 4½" for sashing strip ends

(Cutting List continued on page 54)

THE LILIES (73" X 85"), MADE BY SHARON NEWMAN, QUILTED BY TRECIA SPENCER, LUBBOCK, TEXAS. Geometric patchwork and the graphics of indigo and white equate a dramatic design. The blocks of this quilt are easily prepared with rotary cutting and machine speed piecing.

The Lilies

FIGURE 1. Make 216 half-square units.

corner
triangle

side
triangle

FIGURE 2. Make four columns of six blocks.

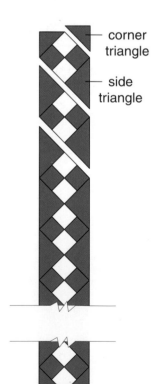

corner
triangle

side
triangle

FIGURE 3. Make three columns of 17 Four-Patches.

(Cutting List continued)

WHITE-ON-WHITE PRINT:
6 strips 2" x 40" for the Four-Patch blocks

108 squares 2⅜" x 2⅜" for half-square units

24 squares 3⅞" x 3⅞", cut once diagonally, for units A and B

24 squares 3½" x 3½" for Unit C

24 stems 1¹⁄₁₆" x 7" (template, page 55)

12 squares 1⅝" x 1⅝" for Unit D, cut once diagonally

10 squares 14" x 14", cut twice diagonally, for side triangles

8 squares 7¼" x 7¼", cut once diagonally, for corner triangles

SEWING DIRECTIONS

MAKING THE LILIES

✦ With right sides together, pair a 2⅜" white square with a 2⅜" indigo square. Draw a diagonal line, corner to corner, on the white square. Sew ¼" from each side of the line and then cut on the line. Press allowances toward the dark to make two half-square units. Make 216 half-square units (Figure 1).

✦ Refer to the block assembly diagrams to make 24 of each of units A, B, C, and D.

ASSEMBLING THE QUILT TOP

✦ Arrange four columns of blocks, side triangles, and corner triangles as shown (Figure 2).

✦ Sew the 2" indigo and 2" white strips in pairs. Press seam allowances toward the dark. Cut the strips into 2" segments. Piece the strips into Four-Patch blocks. Make 51 blocks.

✦ Arrange three columns of 17 Four Patches, side triangles, and corner triangles as shown (Figure 3).

✦ Sew the 1¾" x 4½" strips at the top and bottom of each Four-Patch sashing strip.

✦ Sew the sashing strips between the columns of Lily blocks.

✦ Add borders to all four sides, ending the seams ¼" away from the corners. Miter the corners.

FINISHING THE QUILT

✦ Mark a quilting design. The pieced sashing on THE LILIES is quilted with a zigzag line over the squares. The white background is quilted with a continuous line motif and the Lily blocks are comprised of ovals in the larger triangles, with the other elements outlined.

✦ Layer the quilt top, batting, and backing. Baste.

✦ Quilt and bind.

✦ Sign and date your quilt.

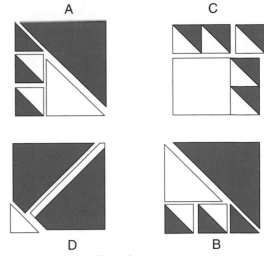

UNIT ASSEMBLY

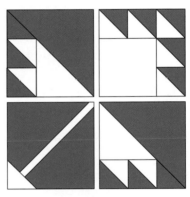

BLOCK ASSEMBLY

THE LILIES stem template

QUILTING DESIGN

Using Templates

Fleur de Nuit

Quilt size 60" x 72½"

FABRIC REQUIREMENTS
BACKGROUND:
4¼ yards black

FLOWERS, SASHING, AND BINDING:
⅓ yard each of 8 different floral prints
½ yard light floral print

BACKING:
4½ yards

CUTTING LIST
BLACK:
2 strips 12½" x 73"
2 strips 15½" x 73"

FLORAL PRINTS:
18 strips 2½" x 21" from each fabric, randomly cut into 2½" x 2½" squares and 2½" x 3½" rectangles
12 petal templates (page 59) from each floral print
32 petal templates (page 59) from the light floral print

FLEUR de NUIT (61" x 72½"), PIECED AND APPLIQUÉD BY SHARON NEWMAN, MACHINE QUILTED BY GAYLE WALLACE, TAYLOR, LOUISIANA. Pastel floral prints on a black background give a whole new look to a familiar design. This quilt was inspired by an Amish Dresden Plate from the 1940s and it is double sided. The reverse side is PINK RECTANGLES on page 59.

Fleur de Nuit

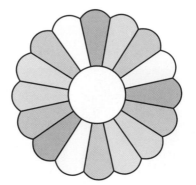

FIGURE 1. Make eight flowers of 16 petals.

FIGURE 2. Press the fabric onto the pressing template.

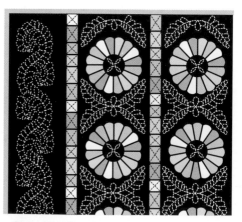

QUILTING DESIGN

SEWING DIRECTIONS

PIECING THE FLOWERS

◆ Sew the flower template pieces into circles, placing the light floral print every fourth piece. Stitch directly on the sewing line, not into the seam allowance. Make eight circles with 16 template pieces each (Figure 1).

◆ Cut a cardboard pressing template from the pattern on page 59. Position the pressing template within the seams on the back of the circles and press the curved edges of the circles over the pressing template to turn under a ¼" allowance (Figure 2).

◆ Place a circle 4¾" from the top and from the bottom, centered in the width of each 15½" black strip. Position the middle two circles 5¾" from the outside circles and 5¾" apart. Appliqué the circles to the background with blind stitches.

PIECING THE COLUMNS AND BINDING

◆ Refer to the photograph on page 57 and piece three sashing strips 73" long, alternating the squares and rectangles.

◆ Piece additional squares and rectangles for the binding. Make two strips 76" long and two strips 64" long.

ASSEMBLING THE QUILT TOP

◆ Sew the two narrow black strips to the pieced sashing strips to make the side panels.

◆ Sew the remaining pieced sashing strip between the appliquéd panels to make the center panel.

◆ Join the side panels to the center panel to complete the quilt top.

FINISHING THE QUILT

✦ Mark a quilting design. Variegated thread was used in FLEUR DE NUIT to machine quilt the large curved feathers in the side panels and the feathers encircling the appliqués. Echo quilting was added in black thread. The appliquéd circles are outlined, and X's are quilted over the patchwork strips.

✦ Layer the quilt top, batting, and backing. Baste.

✦ Quilt and bind.

✦ Sign and date your quilt.

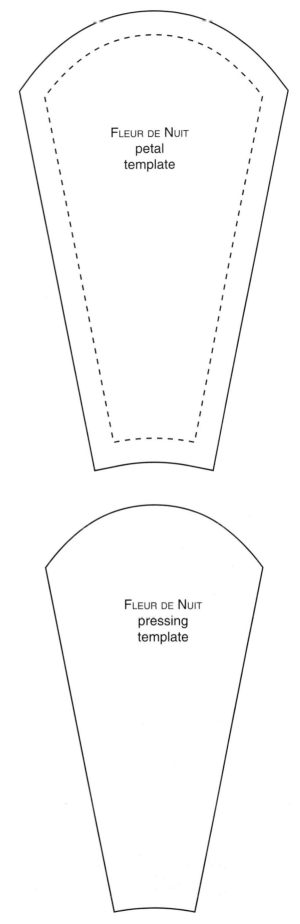

FLEUR DE NUIT
petal
template

FLEUR DE NUIT
pressing
template

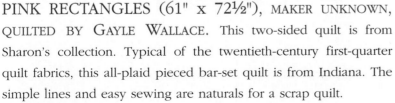

PINK RECTANGLES (61" x 72½"), MAKER UNKNOWN, QUILTED BY GAYLE WALLACE. This two-sided quilt is from Sharon's collection. Typical of the twentieth-century first-quarter quilt fabrics, this all-plaid pieced bar-set quilt is from Indiana. The simple lines and easy sewing are naturals for a scrap quilt.

MORE VERTICAL QUILTS WITH STYLE – BOBBIE A. AUG & SHARON NEWMAN

Colorado Tumbling Blocks

Quilt size 55" x 86"
Block size 9" x 10½" (in length)

FABRIC REQUIREMENTS

BACKGROUND:

1¾ yards

BLOCKS:

¾ yard dark

¾ yard medium

¾ yard light

BORDERS AND SASHING:

4¼ yards floral stripe

Binding:

½ yard

BACKING:

4¾ yards

CUTTING LIST

BORDERS:

2 strips 7½" x 57½" for top and bottom

2 strips 7½" x 90" for sides

SASHING:

2 strips 7½" x 72¼"

BLOCKS:

21 dark Template A

21 medium Template A

21 light Template A

BACKGROUND:

36 Template B (½ diamond)

12 Template C (¼ diamond)

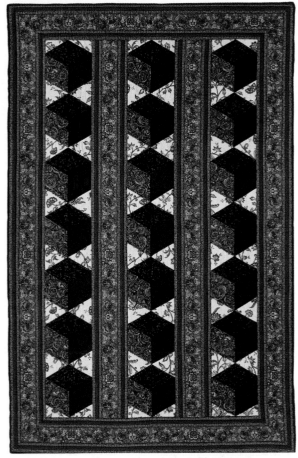

COLORADO TUMBLING BLOCKS (53½" x 84¼"), MADE BY BOBBIE AUG, QUILTED BY SANDI FRUEHLING, AURORA, COLORADO. Always a favorite, this pieced block has a whole different look when set in bars. The three-dimensional effect is captured in these large blocks and they can easily be pieced by hand or machine.

Colorado Tumbling Blocks

FIGURE 1. Sew a dark A to a medium A.

FIGURE 2. Sew a light A to a medium A.

FIGURE 3. Sew the dark A to the light A.

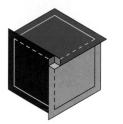

FIGURE 4. Press seam allowances clockwise.

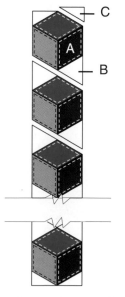

FIGURE 5. Make three columns of seven blocks.

SEWING DIRECTIONS

PIECING THE BLOCKS

Maintaining the pattern of light, medium, and dark, make 21 blocks as described in the following steps:

✦ Sew a dark A to a medium A by matching the diamonds exactly and sewing on the drawn seam line (Figure 1). Be careful not to sew into the seam allowances when joining diamonds.

✦ For the second seam, pull the dark diamond out of the way while aligning the medium and light diamonds with right sides together. Match all the edges of the medium and light diamonds, not just the side to be sewn. Sew the light A to the medium A (Figure 2).

✦ For the third seam, pull the medium diamond out of the way as you align the dark and light diamonds with right sides together. Match all of the edges of the dark and light diamonds, not just the side to be sewn. Sew the dark A to the light A on the seam line only (Figure 3).

✦ Press the seam allowances for the blocks clockwise, opening the seam allowance intersection as shown (Figure 4).

PIECING THE COLUMNS

✦ Arrange three columns of seven blocks.

✦ Add B pieces to create straight edges on each side of the blocks as shown (Figure 5).

✦ Add C pieces to create straight edges on the top and bottom of each vertical column.

ASSEMBLING THE QUILT TOP

✦ Mark the sashing strips with a ¼" seam allowance at each end and at 10" intervals.

✦ Match and pin diamond points to the grid marks on the sashing and sew together sashing and columns. Press.

✦ Add borders to all four sides, ending the seams ¼" away from the corners. Miter the corners.

FINISHING THE QUILT

✦ Mark a quilting design. The border on COLORADO TUMBLING BLOCKS is quilted mirroring the floral print. Straight lines follow the stripe in the border. The triangles are quilted in the ditch and the diamonds are quilted ¼" inside the seam line.

✦ Layer the quilt top, batting, and backing. Baste.

✦ Quilt and bind.

✦ Sign and date your quilt.

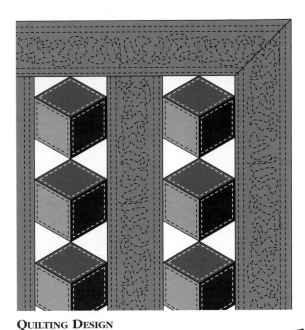

QUILTING DESIGN

A

COLORADO
TUMBLING
BLOCKS

B

COLORADO
TUMBLING
BLOCKS
½ DIAMOND

C

COLORADO
TUMBLING
BLOCK
¼ DIAMOND

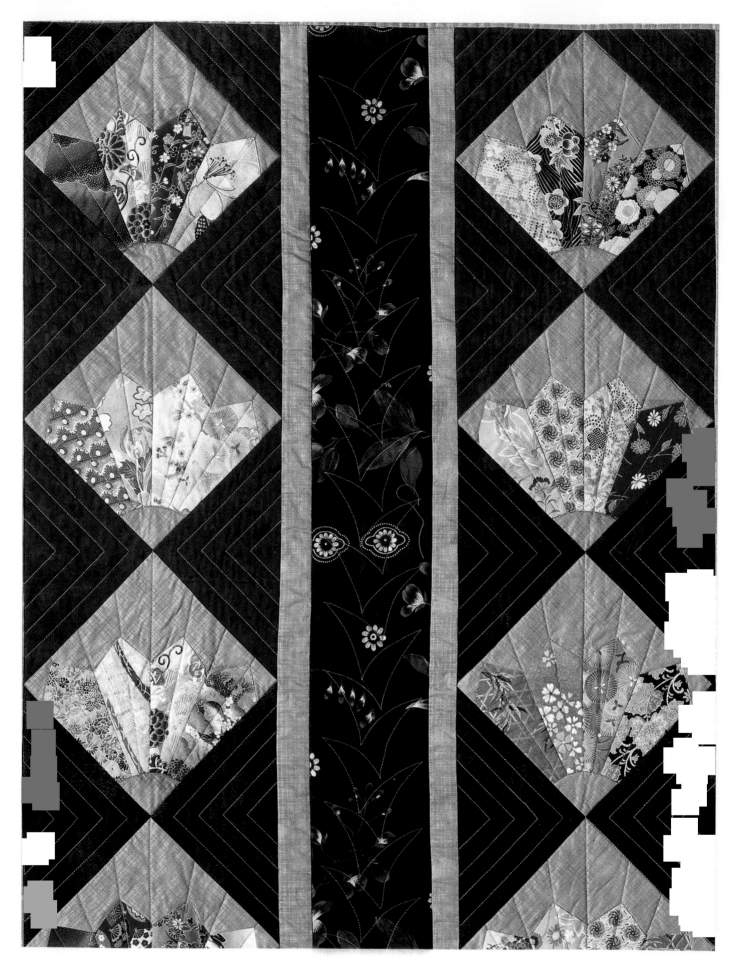

More Vertical Quilts with Style – Bobbie A. Aug & Sharon Newman

Fans

Quilt size 67" x 75½"
Block size 8½" x 8½"

These instructions are for fans pieced by machine and appliquéd by using a machine straight stitch. However, any pattern and method desired can be used for making the fans.

FABRIC REQUIREMENTS

SASHING AND BORDERS:

2 yards dark floral print

BACKGROUND, SASHING, BORDERS, AND BINDING:

2¾ yards gold print

SIDE AND CORNER TRIANGLES:

⅔ yard black print
⅔ yard purple print

FANS:

12 or more prints totaling 1½ yards

BACKING:

4 yards (seam horizontally)

CUTTING LIST

DARK FLORAL:

4 strips 5¾" x 60½" for sashing and side borders
2 strips 5¾" x 67½" for top and bottom borders

GOLD PRINT:

15 squares 9" x 9" for background
8 strips 1¾" x 62" for sashing units
4 strips 1¾" x 70" for top and bottom borders

BLACK PRINT:

3 squares 13¼" x 13¼", cut twice diagonally

3 squares 6⅞" x 6⅞", cut once diagonally

(Cutting List continued on page 66)

FANS (67" x 75¼"), MADE BY BOBBIE AUG AND QUILTED BY SANDI FRUEHLING, AURORA, COLORADO. In the 1980s, Bobbie and her friend Carla Hale spent many days exploring a variety of ways to make fan patterns. They shared a love for the romance of this block design. The most appealing aspect of this design was that each block could display many different prints in a very elegant manner. This beloved pattern was highlighted in this quilt by placing the blocks in a vertical set.

Fans

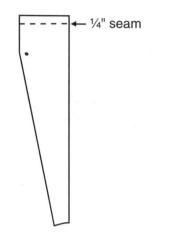

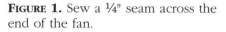

← ¼" seam

FIGURE 1. Sew a ¼" seam across the end of the fan.

corner triangle

side triangle

FIGURE 2. Make three columns of 5 blocks.

QUILTING DESIGN

PURPLE PRINT:

3 squares 13¼" x 13¼", cut twice diagonally

3 squares 6⅞" x 6⅞", cut once diagonally

FAN PRINTS:

Cut a total of 60 fan-blade templates (page 67) from a variety of prints. These can be rotary cut on three sides by cutting 4¼" strips and then cutting the strips into the fan-blade templates.

MARKING THE FAN BLADES

Trace the fan blade on template plastic, marking the straight- grainline and dots. Use a ⅛" hole punch or a sharp pointed object, such as the end of a compass to make a small hole where each dot is marked. Transfer the dots with a non-permanent marking pen or pencil on the wrong side of each fan-blade fabric piece.

SEWING DIRECTIONS

PIECING THE BLOCKS

◆ Fold one fan blade in half lengthwise, right sides together, and lightly press. With a ¼" seam allowance, sew across the end of the fan as shown (Figure 1). Turn the fan right side out and position the seam along the center back of the fan blade. Press. Repeat this step for all 60 fan blades.

◆ Using complimentary prints, sew fan blades into pairs, beginning at the dot and sewing the lengthwise seam. Press. Make 30 pairs.

◆ Join pairs to form a unit of four fan blades. Press. Make 15 units.

◆ Press a ¼" allowance under on the lower edges of the fans. Position the fans on the background square as shown in the photo on page 65. Pin or baste the fans in place on the background blocks.

◆ Using a .004 (not craft weight) nylon filament thread on

top and a regular sewing thread in the bobbin, straight stitch the fan points in place 1⁄16" from the outer edge. Stitch the curved edge by using the same method. Make 15 blocks. If you plan on hand quilting, you may want to trim the background fabric from behind the fans.

PIECING THE COLUMNS

✦ Arrange three columns of blocks, side triangles, and corner triangles as shown (Figure 2, page 66).

ASSEMBLING THE QUILT TOP

✦ Sew a gold sashing strip to each long side of a dark floral sashing strip to make a sashing unit. Press. Make four units.

✦ Mark sashing units with a 1⁄4" seam allowance at each end and at 11⅝" intervals. Match and pin block points to marks on sashing units. Sew together sashing units and block strips, beginning and ending with a sashing unit. Press.

✦ Sew a gold border strip to each long side of the two dark floral border strips to make the top and bottom border units. Press. Join these units to the quilt top. Press.

FINISHING THE QUILT

✦ Mark a quilting design. For this quilt, the triangles are quilted in lines forming triangles 3⁄4" apart. The fans are quilted in radiating lines through the center of each fan blade and extending to the outer edge of each block. A bamboo design is used in each of the bars and borders.

✦ Layer the quilt top, batting, and backing. Baste.

✦ Quilt and bind.

✦ Sign and date your quilt.

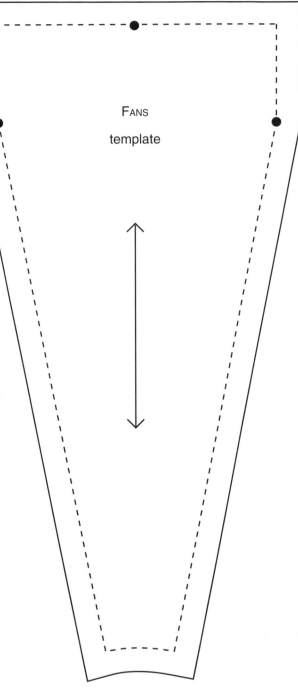

FANS

template

MORE VERTICAL QUILTS WITH STYLE – BOBBIE A. AUG & SHARON NEWMAN

Spring Morning

Quilt size 32" x 38"
Block size 7¼" x 7¼"

FABRIC REQUIREMENTS

BLOCKS:

⅛ yard green print
⅛ yard dark red print
⅛ yard dark mauve print
⅛ yard peach print
⅛ yard yellow print

BLOCK BACKGROUND:

¼ yard cream

BACKGROUND:

⅝ yard blue

BORDERS, SASHING, AND BINDING:

1 yard

BACKING:

1 yard

ADDITIONAL MATERIALS

Freezer paper
Template plastic

CUTTING LIST

BLOCK PRINTS:

Make templates from the patterns on pages 71 and 72. Using the photo as a guide for color placement, use each template to cut six fabric pieces.

BLUE BACKGROUND:

⊠ 2 squares 11¼" x 11¼", cut twice diagonally, for side triangles

◺ 4 squares 6" x 6", cut once diagonally, for corner triangles

(Cutting List continued on page 70)

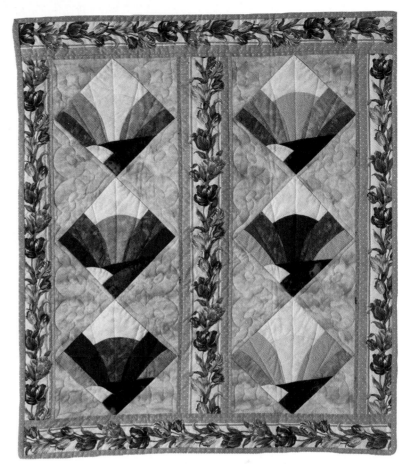

SPRING MORNING (30½" x 35¼"), MADE BY SHARON NEWMAN AND QUILTED BY SANDRA BENNETT, LUBBOCK, TEXAS. This pieced quilt was made from an Alice Brooks pattern called Grandmother's Favorite (#1044). The tulip fabric in the borders and sashing has a glazed finish.

Spring Morning

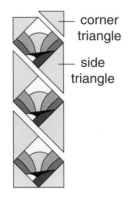

FIGURE 1. Make two columns of three blocks.

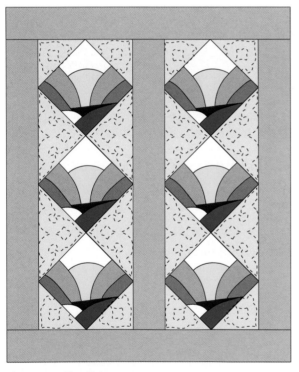

QUILTING DESIGN

(Cutting List continued)

BORDERS AND SASHING:
1 strip 4¾" x 31¼" for sashing
2 strips 4" x 31¼" for side borders
2 strips 4" x 38½" for top and bottom borders

SEWING DIRECTIONS

PIECING THE BLOCKS

✦ Trace the templates on pages 71 and 72 on freezer paper and retrace the templates and hatch marks on plain or gridded template plastic. Cut out the plastic templates and use them to mark the fabrics. Add ¼" seam allowances by eye as you cut.

✦ Refer to the block assembly diagram on page 73 and make six blocks.

PIECING THE COLUMNS

✦ Arrange two columns of blocks, side triangles, and corner triangles, as shown (Figure 1).

ASSEMBLING THE QUILT TOP

✦ Fold and mark the sashing strip at the half point. Match the corners of the center blocks with the half mark on the sashing. Sew the sashing strip between the columns.

✦ Sew the side borders to the quilt top. Press.

✦ Add the top and bottom borders to complete the quilt top. Press.

FINISHING THE QUILT

✦ Mark a quilting design. A stylized motif was the basis for the quilting design used in SPRING MORNING. Refer to page 73 for the pattern.

✦ Layer the quilt top, batting, and backing. Baste.

✦ Quilt and bind. Note: This quilt has a two-sided binding.

✦ Sign and date your quilt.

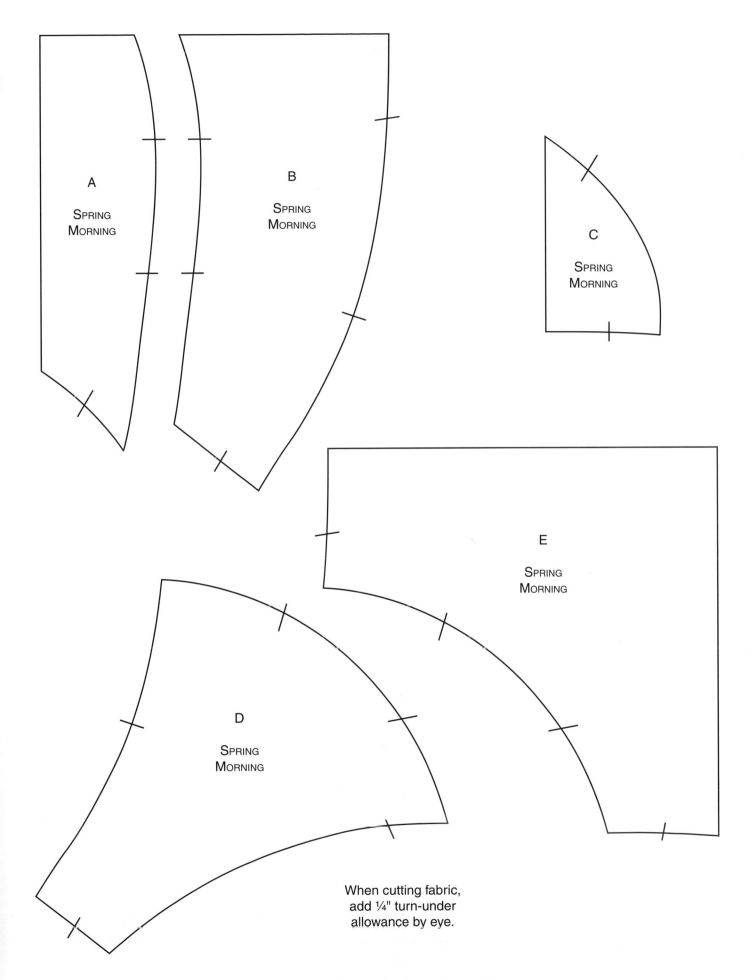

A

SPRING
MORNING

B

SPRING
MORNING

C

SPRING
MORNING

E

SPRING
MORNING

D

SPRING
MORNING

When cutting fabric,
add ¼" turn-under
allowance by eye.

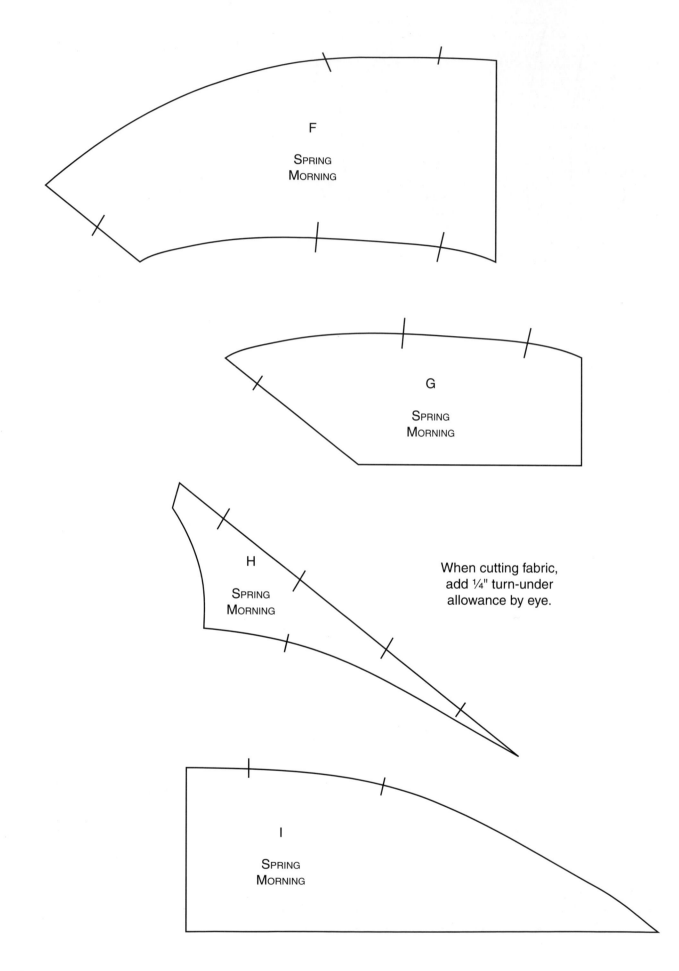

F

SPRING
MORNING

G

SPRING
MORNING

H

SPRING
MORNING

When cutting fabric,
add ¼" turn-under
allowance by eye.

I

SPRING
MORNING

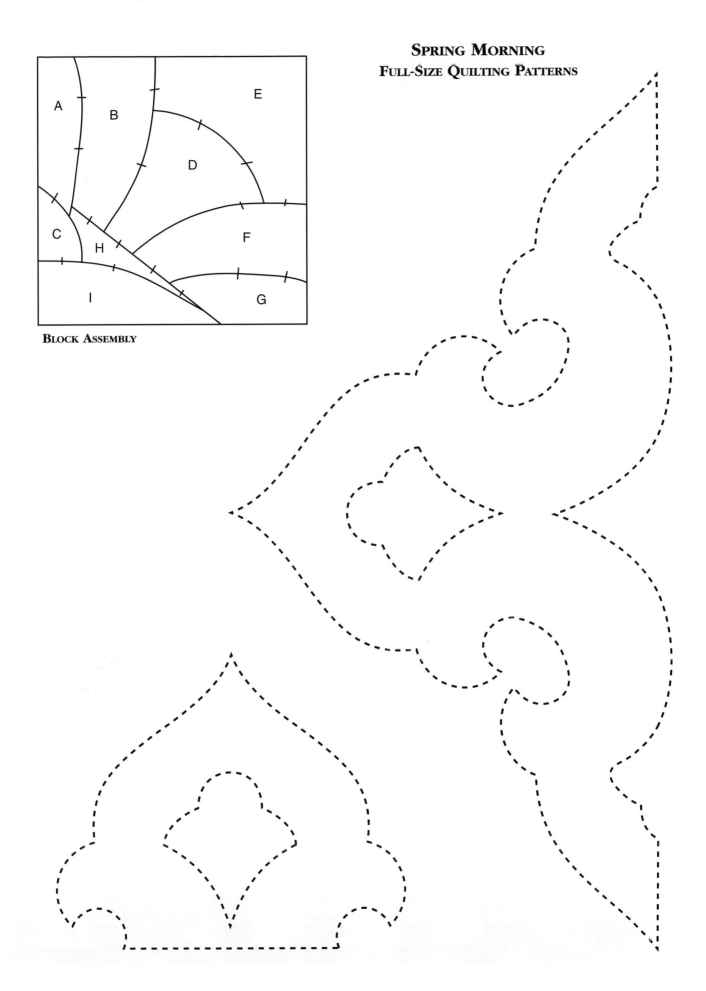

BLOCK ASSEMBLY

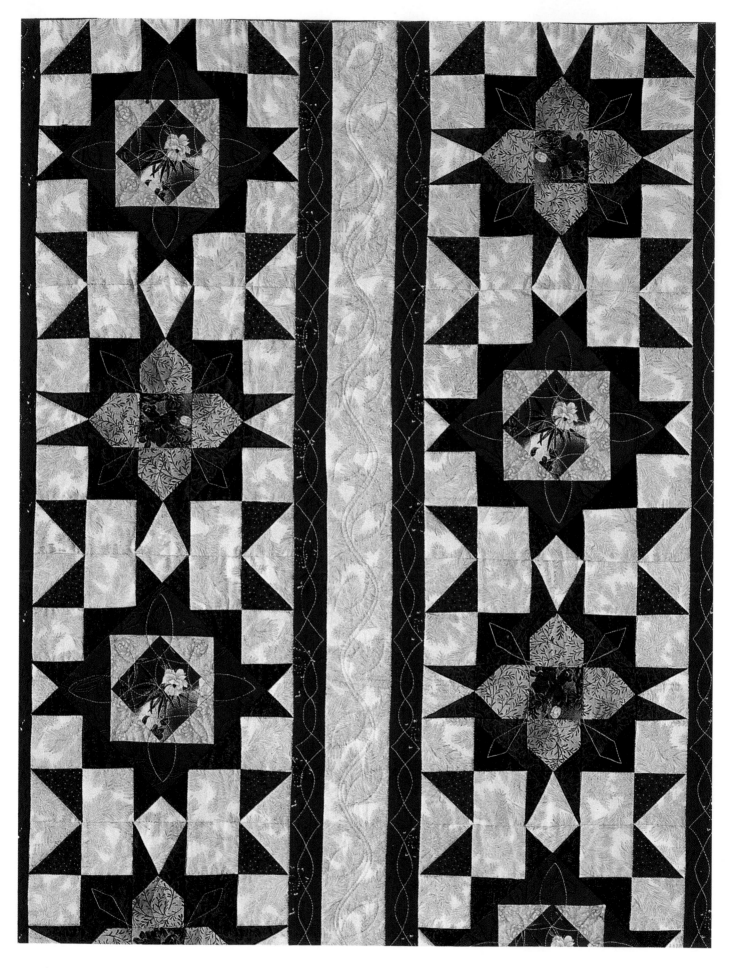

More Vertical Quilts with Style – Bobbie A. Aug & Sharon Newman

California Constellation

Quilt size 55½" x 68½"
Block size: 12½" x 12½"

FABRIC REQUIREMENTS

BORDERS, SASHING, AND BINDING:

2¼ yards red

BACKGROUND AND SASHING:

2¼ yards gold

ACCENT CENTERS:

⅓ yard large floral print

BLOCKS:

⅜ yard large red print
⅜ yard each of two peach prints
⅜ yard small red print
¾ yard green print
¾ yard blue print

BACKING:

3½ yards

CUTTING LIST

RED:

2 strips 3½" x 70" for side borders
2 strips 3½" x 57½" for top and
    bottom borders
4 strips 2" x 63" for sashing

GOLD:

2 strips 3½" x 63" for sashing
120 squares 3" x 3" (D)

⬜ 30 squares 3⅜" x 3⅜" (B), cut once
    diagonally

⬜ 8 squares 3¾" x 3¾" (E), cut twice
    diagonally

28 Template I

(Cutting List continued on page 76)

CALIFORNIA CONSTELLATION (52" x 65"), PIECED
BY SHARON NEWMAN AND MACHINE QUILTED BY SARA
VOYLES, LUBBOCK, TEXAS. The fabrics used in this quilt were
acquired by Sharon during a trip to California. The two-block
design is from a series called Baker's Dozen by Jackie Reis, who
has been a sampler quilt teacher for 20 years.

California Constellation

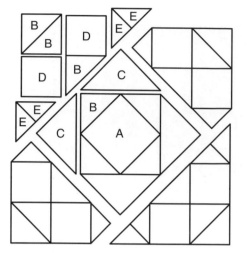

BLOCK I ASSEMBLY

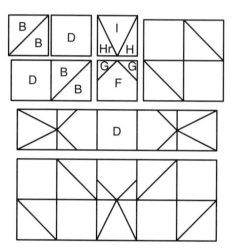

BLOCK II ASSEMBLY

QUILTING DESIGN

(Cutting List continued)

LARGE FLORAL PRINT:
8 squares 4" x 4" (patch A)
7 squares 3" x 3" (D)

PEACH PRINTS:
16 squares 3⅜" x 3⅜" (B) of one print, cut once diagonally
28 Template F of the other print

LARGE RED PRINT:
32 Template C

SMALL RED PRINT:
30 squares 3⅜" x 3⅜" (B), cut once diagonally

GREEN PRINT:
30 squares 3⅜" x 3⅜" (B), cut once diagonally
16 squares 3¾" x 3¾" (E), cut twice diagonally

BLUE PRINT:
14 squares 3⅜" x 3⅜" (B), cut once diagonally
28 squares 2⅛" x 2⅛" (G), cut once diagonally
28 Template H
28 Template Hr

SEWING DIRECTIONS

PIECING BLOCK I
✦ Refer to the block assembly diagram and make eight blocks.

PIECING BLOCK II
✦ Refer to the block assembly diagram and make seven blocks.

ASSEMBLING THE QUILT TOP
✦ Arrange the blocks in three columns, alternating the two blocks. Sew the blocks in straight seams.

✦ Sew red sashing strips on each side of the gold sashing strips.

✦ Assemble the columns and sashing starting and ending with the columns

✦ Add borders to all four sides ending the seams ¼" away from the corners. Miter the corners.

FINISHING THE QUILT:

✦ Mark a quilting design. This quilt is machine quilted in outlines of the patchwork with designs (pages 78 and 79) over the blocks. The gold sashing is quilted in a vine-and-leaf design and the red sashing is an egg-and-diamond motif. The border is quilted in looping designs.

✦ Layer the quilt top, batting, and backing. Baste.

✦ Quilt and bind.

✦ Sign and date your quilt.

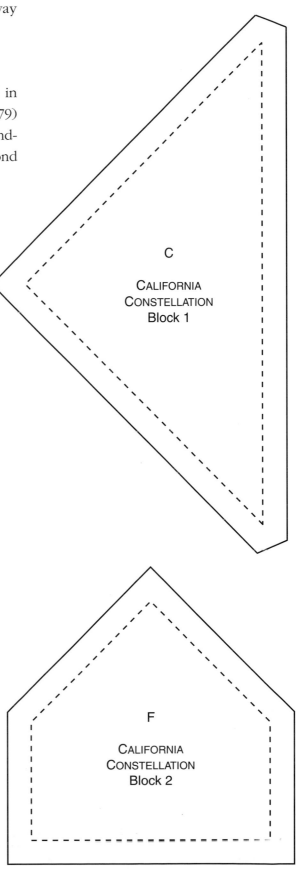

C

CALIFORNIA
CONSTELLATION
Block 1

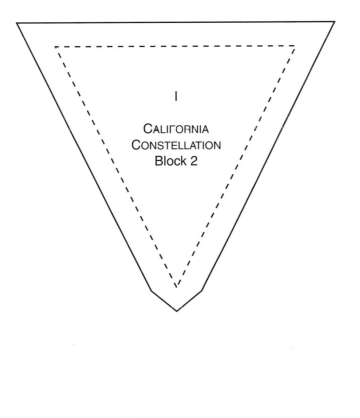

I

CALIFORNIA
CONSTELLATION
Block 2

F

CALIFORNIA
CONSTELLATION
Block 2

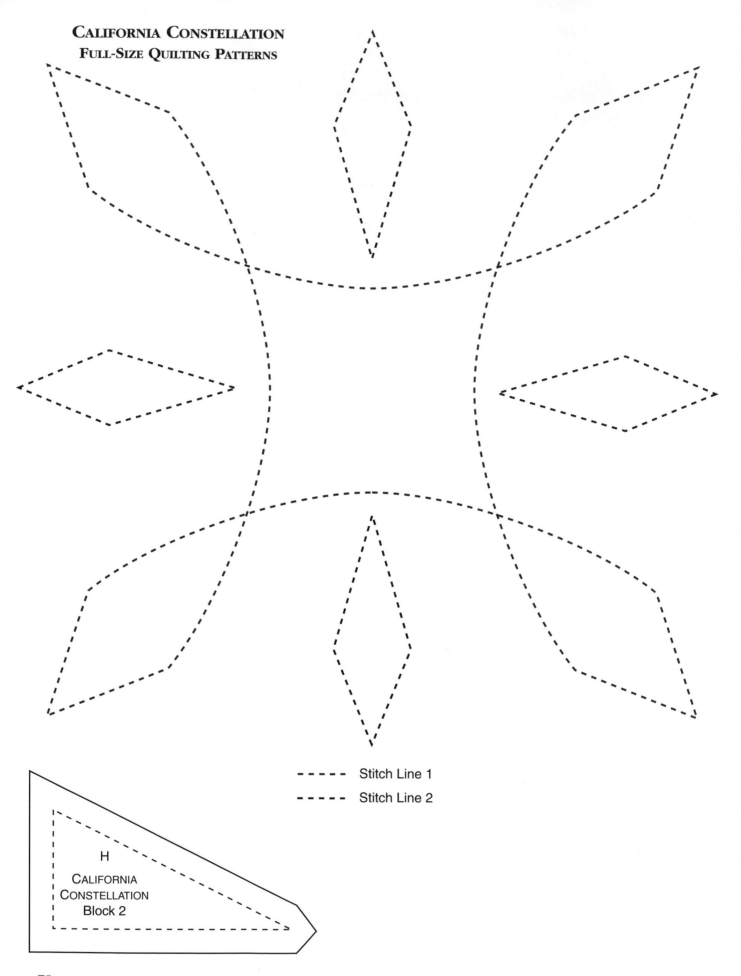

- - - - Stitch Line 1

- - - - Stitch Line 2

H

CALIFORNIA
CONSTELLATION
Block 2

MORE VERTICAL QUILTS WITH STYLE – BOBBIE A. AUG & SHARON NEWMAN

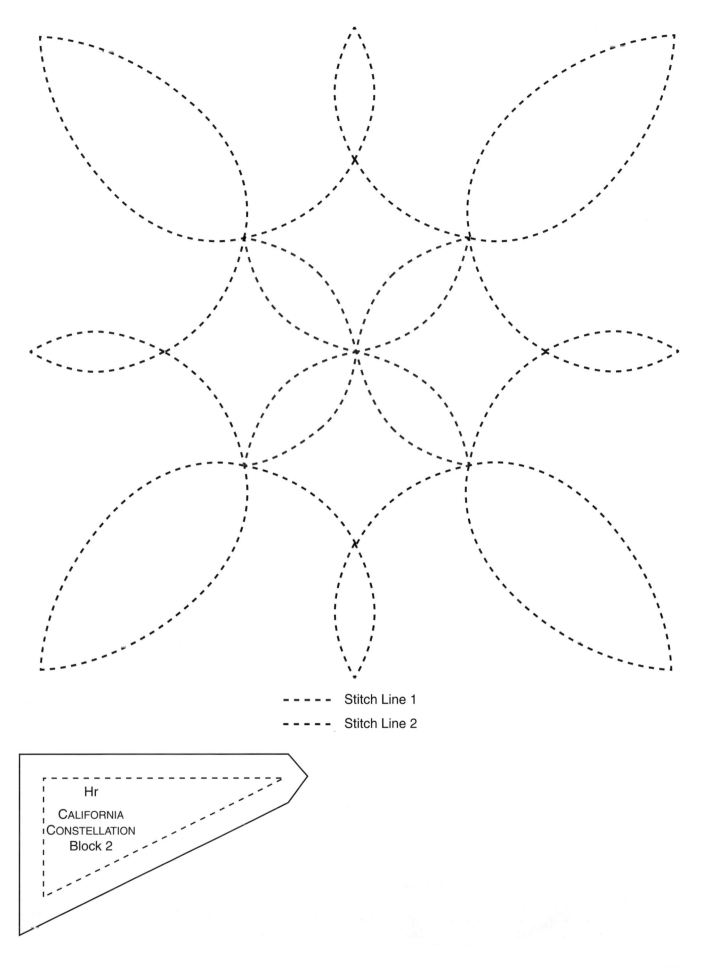

- - - - Stitch Line 1

- - - - Stitch Line 2

Hr

CALIFORNIA
CONSTELLATION
Block 2

Lady Bird's Rose Garden

Quilt size 57" x 72"

FABRIC REQUIREMENTS
APPLIQUÉ BACKGROUND: 2¼ yards solid color

SASHING: 2¼ yards print

LEAVES: ¾ yard assorted greens

STEMS: ½ yard

BIRDS: assorted fat quarters for two different birds

FLOWERS: assorted fat quarters for different flowers

BACKING: 4½ yards

BINDING: ½ yard

ADDITIONAL MATERIALS:
Cotton thread
Embroidery floss
Embroidery needle
Fine sandpaper, one sheet
Fine silk pins, headless
Freezer paper
Mechanical pencil
Rotary cutter, ruler, and mat
(Refer to the Resources section, page 95)

CUTTING LIST
APPLIQUÉ BACKGROUND:
2 strips 11" x 2¼ yards for appliqué panels (will be trimmed to 10" x 72½")

SASHING:
4 strips 10" x 72½"
Differences in the fabrics chosen for these panels may create changes in the width. Use of border prints will determine the width.

SEWING DIRECTIONS

PREPARING THE PATTERN PIECES

✦ Photocopy the appliqué patterns and cut them out. Cut a piece of paper the finished size of the sash. Fold the paper in half lengthwise and crosswise to mark the centers to use as placement guides for the left panel. For the left panel, draw the vine free-hand on the paper and place the cut-out appliqué patterns as desired on the vines. Trace around the patterns as many times as needed to complete the sash. Make a second copy of the sash, reversing the images to produce the second sash.

✦ Place the sash patterns side by side, aligning the motifs. Tape the pattern together. Place the background fabric right side up over the top of the sash patterns. Move to a light source if the design is not visible through the fabric. Center and pin the fabric to the patterns to prevent movement.

✦ To indicate where the appliqué pieces should be positioned on the background, you can make locator marks instead of marking the pattern lines on the background fabric. For example, mark one line along the center of a stem and use small points at the tips of the leaves, just inside the pattern line. To avoid marking entirely, you can baste the appliqué pieces directly on the background fabric.

✦ If you prefer to make freezer-paper templates for cutting the appliqué pieces, trace the leaves and flowers on the dull side of the freezer paper. Transfer the pattern numbers and letters to the freezer paper. The letter "L" is for the left panel pattern pieces. Mark the right panel pattern pieces with the letter "R."

LADY BIRD'S ROSE GARDEN (50½" x 72"), MADE BY DARLENE C. CHRISTOPHERSON, CHINA SPRING, TEXAS, AND QUILTED BY JUDY STEWARD, HEWITT, TEXAS. Sharon and Darlene were roommates during a quilt conference in 1998. After viewing Sharon's bar-set quilts, Darlene began searching for fabric to create an appliqué version of one. She found a reproduction print at a vendor's mall for the sashing and fashioned shapes into a pair of mirror-images for the appliqué panels.

Darlene is an accomplished quiltmaker and instructor, who freely shares her experiences and knowledge with groups and symposiums nationwide. Refer to the Resources section, page 95, for contact information.

Lady Bird's Rose Garden

BIAS STEMS

To pin, place fine silk pins through the bias stem at a right angle, catching a small part of the stem as shown. When basting the stems in place, take one stitch on the right side of the stem and one stitch on the left side and so on. You are merely fastening the pieces in place, not turning the raw edges as you baste. Neatness and consistency in trimming the allowance and basting is key to your comfort while working and to the end result achieved.

EMBROIDERY STITCHES

Stem stitch: Bring the needle up at the beginning of the line to be covered. Insert the needle a short distance to the right and bring it out a little to the left at a slight angle. Keep the thread above the needle.

French knot: Bring the needle up at a point where the knot is to be made. Wrap the thread two or three times around the point of the needle. Insert it in the fabric as close as possible to the spot where the thread emerges (but not in the exact spot) and pull it to the wrong side, holding the wraps in place.

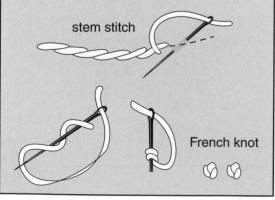

stem stitch

French knot

◆ Cut out the freezer paper templates on the line. Store each panel separately in resealable bags until needed.

PREPARING THE APPLIQUÉ PIECES
◆ Press each paper template, waxy side down, on the right side of the chosen fabric. Leave at least ⅛" turn-under allowance around each piece. You will want to distribute the different green fabrics evenly throughout the pattern.

◆ Using a sharpened silver or white pencil, trace around the paper templates. (Place very fine sandpaper under the fabric to keep the pencil from tugging on the fabric.) It is easier to trace the templates before cutting the pieces out.

◆ In the allowance, mark the sections that will lie under other pieces as a reminder not to turn them under. Cut around each paper template, leaving a ¼" allowance for the underlying pieces and a ⅛" allowance for the areas that will be turned.

PREPARING THE STEMS
◆ Using a rotary cutter, ruler, and mat, cut strips ¾" wide on the bias (at a 45° angle to the straight edge of the fabric). Some of the stems call for a length of at least 24" while others are only 3". The total length of bias for each panel is approximately 135", so cut at least 270" total.

◆ Using a dry, medium-hot iron, press the bias strips in half lengthwise with the right sides out. Then fold in half lengthwise again and press. The folded edge should cover the two raw edges. Use a shot of steam on the second fold to set the crease. Keep the width uniform. Immediately wrap the completed stems around a pincushion and fasten with a pin. Set aside until needed.

PINNING AND BASTING
◆ Place the stems on the background fabric as shown on the pattern and trim to the appropriate length. Pin in place (refer to Bias Stems). Then place each pattern piece, remove the paper template, and pin to the background fabric.

✦ After the stems and all of the pieces have been pinned to both panels, you can remove the pattern layout sheet. Baste with a contrasting thread slightly more than ⅛" from the pencil line.

APPLIQUÉING THE PIECES

✦ Use the needle-turn method or your favorite method to appliqué the flowers, leaves, and stems to the background.

EMBROIDERING THE DETAILS

✦ Use stem stitches and French knots to add details, such as the birds' eyes and any desired tendrils (refer to Embroidery Stitches, page 82). Use embroidery floss and an embroidery needle. If you prefer, you can use a permanent pen to draw the details.

ASSEMBLING THE QUILT TOP

Note: The width of the sashing strips may vary slightly, but stay within 10" to 12". If you are using a border print or stripe, use the lines printed on the fabric as guides, allowing for the ¼" seam allowance. If you are using a large floral or other nondescript print, you may choose to border this fabric with a narrow-striped print on both sides.

✦ Mark sashing strips and appliquéd panels ¼" from the edge at each corner and at half, quarter, and eighth marks.

✦ Arrange the panels and sashing strips, beginning and ending with a sashing strip. Pin and sew the panels and sashing strips together, matching marked points. Press.

FINISHING THE QUILT

✦ Mark a quilting design. LADY BIRD'S ROSE GARDEN is quilted in the ditch around all appliqué pieces and gridded down the background to the panels using diagonal lines, crosshatching, or stippling. The alternate panel fabric can inspire design ideas. Border prints are easy to quilt using the lines they present. A large floral print can also be a great guide to a quilting design.

✦ Layer the quilt top, batting, and backing. Baste.

✦ Quilt and bind.

✦ Sign and date your quilt.

QUILTING DESIGN

After completing the quilt top, Darlene held a contest at a local quilt shop to name her quilt. Many entries were submitted, but LADY BIRD'S ROSE GARDEN was the name suggested by Lynah Engeberger.

4L

LADY BIRD'S ROSE GARDEN

10L

LADY BIRD'S ROSE GARDEN

1L

LADY BIRD'S ROSE GARDEN

2L

LADY BIRD'S ROSE GARDEN

3L

LADY BIRD'S ROSE GARDEN

9L

LADY BIRD'S ROSE GARDEN

When cutting fabric,
leave a ⅛" turn-under
allowance around each piece
(¼" for underlying pieces).

1L

2L

3L

4L

5L

8L

7L

6L

9L

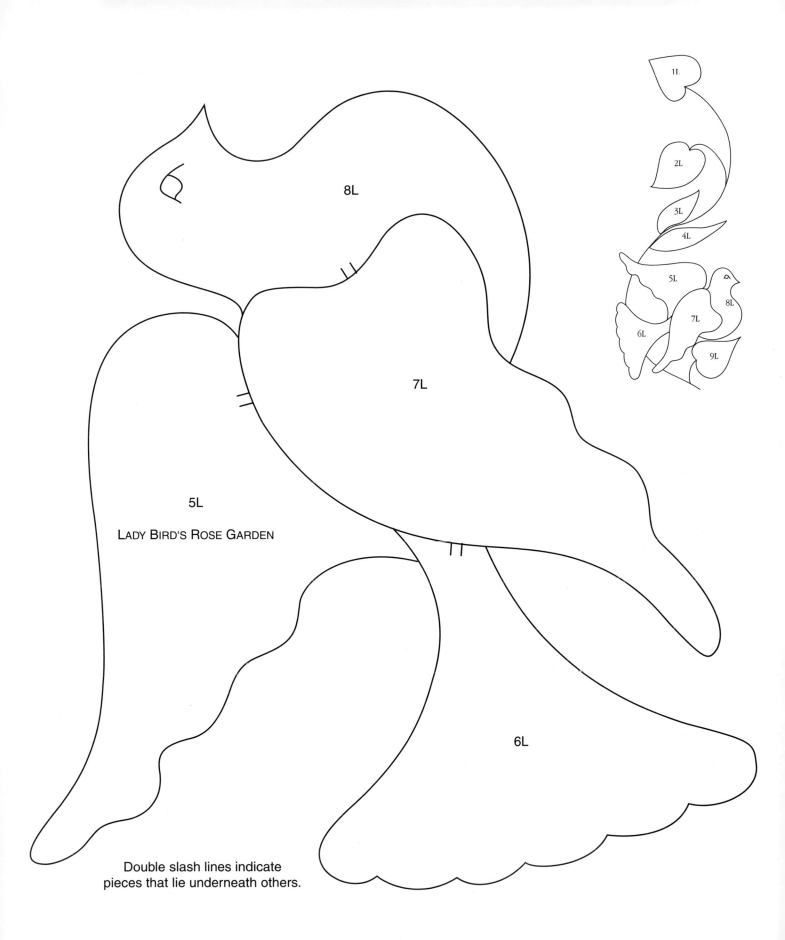

8L

7L

5L

LADY BIRD'S ROSE GARDEN

6L

Double slash lines indicate
pieces that lie underneath others.

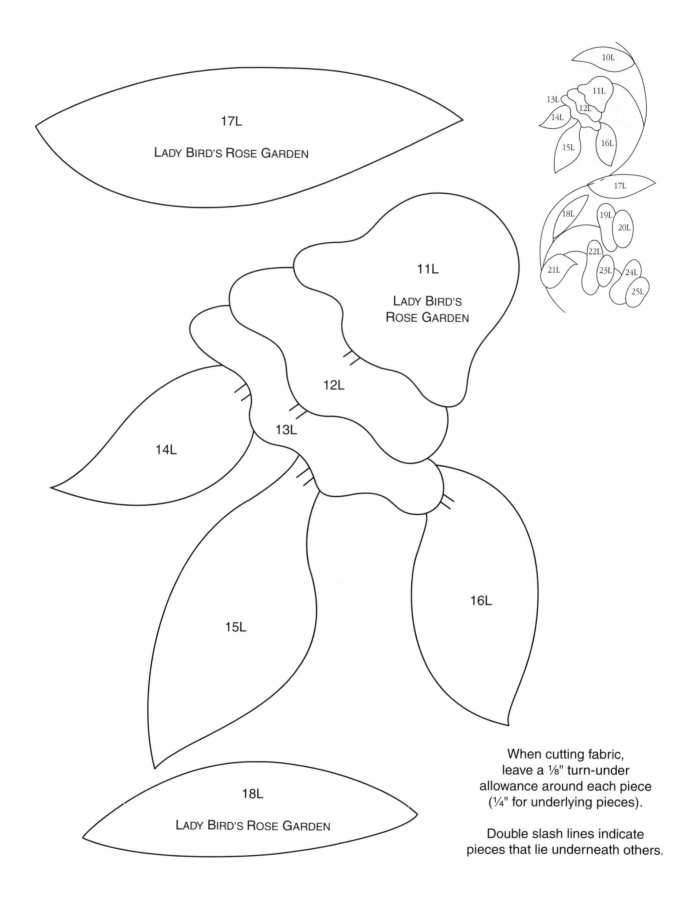

17L

LADY BIRD'S ROSE GARDEN

11L

LADY BIRD'S
ROSE GARDEN

12L

13L

14L

15L

16L

18L

LADY BIRD'S ROSE GARDEN

When cutting fabric,
leave a ⅛" turn-under
allowance around each piece
(¼" for underlying pieces).

Double slash lines indicate
pieces that lie underneath others.

10L

11L

13L

12L

14L

15L

16L

17L

18L

19L

20L

22L

21L

23L

24L

25L

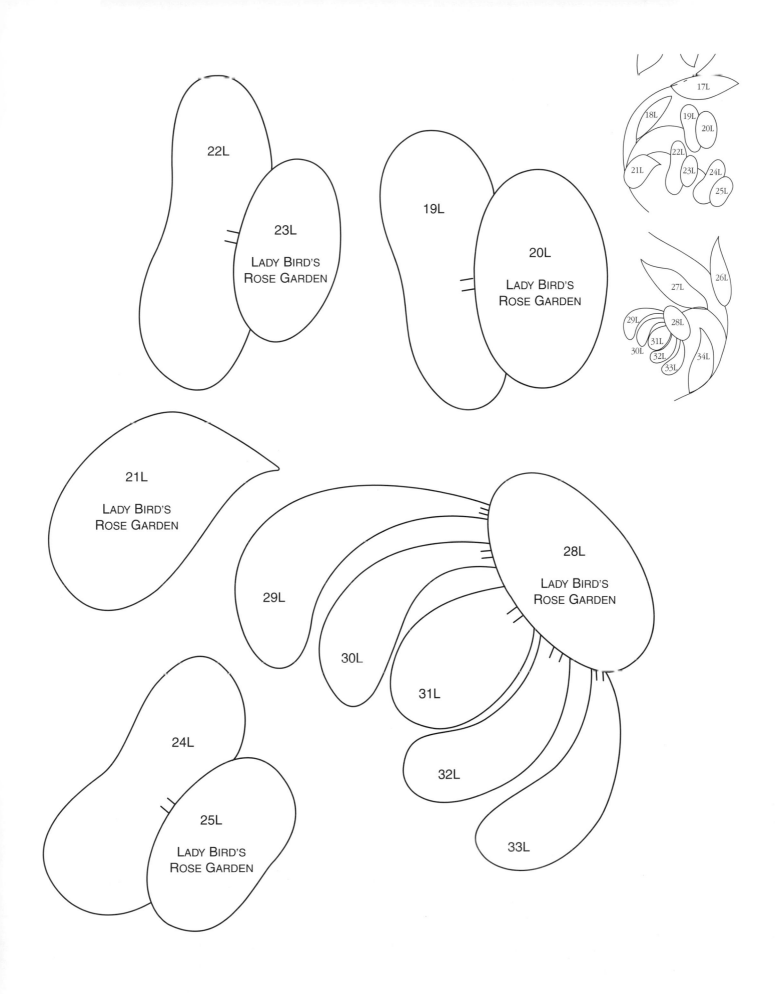

22L

23L
LADY BIRD'S
ROSE GARDEN

19L

20L
LADY BIRD'S
ROSE GARDEN

17L

18L   19L
         20L
      22L
21L   23L   24L
                  25L

26L
27L

29L   28L
30L 31L
    32L   34L
      33L

21L
LADY BIRD'S
ROSE GARDEN

29L

30L

31L

28L
LADY BIRD'S
ROSE GARDEN

24L

25L
LADY BIRD'S
ROSE GARDEN

32L

33L

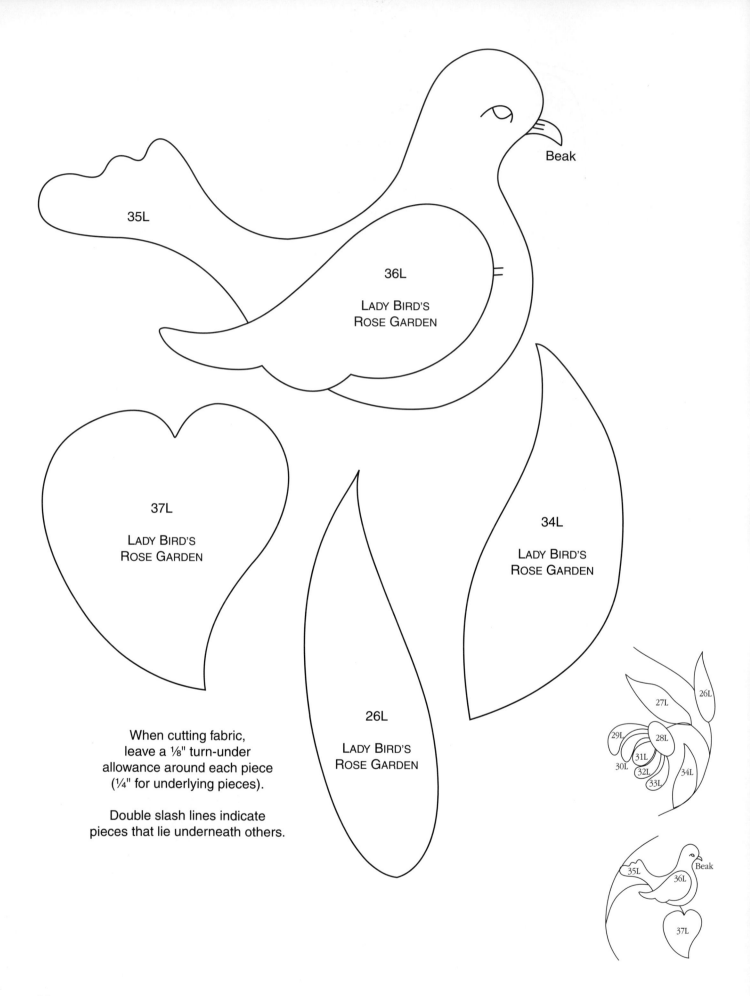

35L

Beak

36L

LADY BIRD'S
ROSE GARDEN

37L

LADY BIRD'S
ROSE GARDEN

34L

LADY BIRD'S
ROSE GARDEN

26L

LADY BIRD'S
ROSE GARDEN

When cutting fabric,
leave a ⅛" turn-under
allowance around each piece
(¼" for underlying pieces).

Double slash lines indicate
pieces that lie underneath others.

26L
27L
29L
28L
31L
30L
32L
34L
33L

35L
36L
Beak
37L

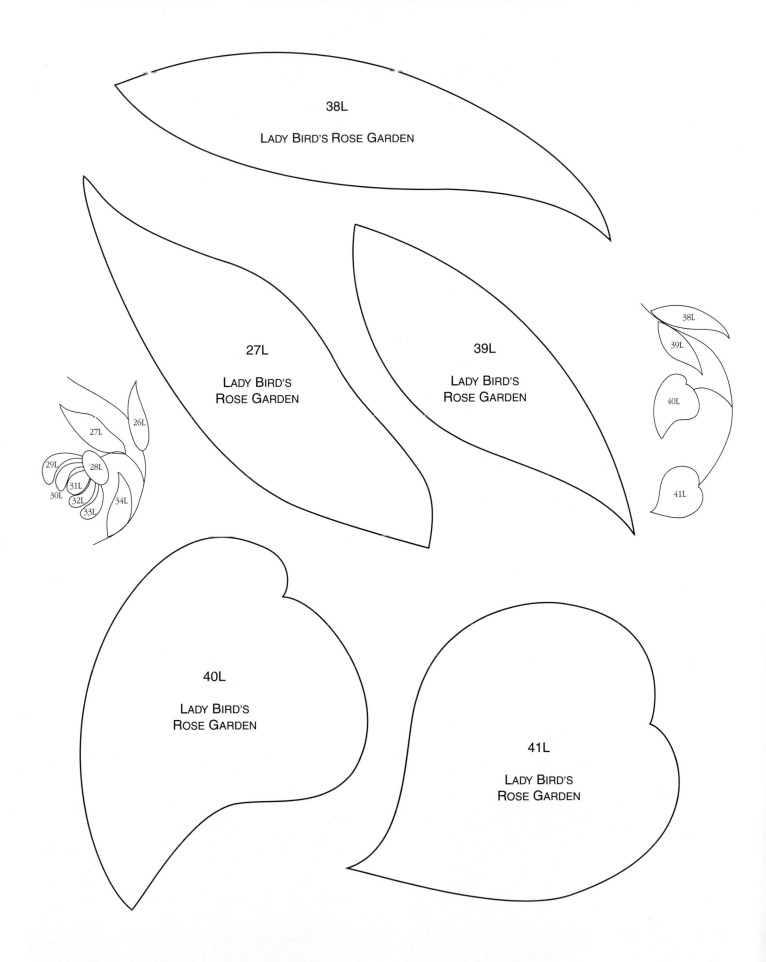

38L

LADY BIRD'S ROSE GARDEN

27L

LADY BIRD'S
ROSE GARDEN

39L

LADY BIRD'S
ROSE GARDEN

38L

39L

40L

41L

26L

27L

29L

28L

31L

30L

32L

33L

34L

40L

LADY BIRD'S
ROSE GARDEN

41L

LADY BIRD'S
ROSE GARDEN

Other Vertical Patterns

Lancaster Mennonite Bars

Quilt size 69½" x 75½"

FABRIC REQUIREMENTS

GREEN BARS: 2¼ yards solid color

YELLOW BARS AND BINDING: 3 yards solid

RED BARS: 2¼ yards solid

BACKING: 4⅜ yards (seam horizontally)

CUTTING LIST

GREEN: 6 strips 6" x 76"

YELLOW: 5 strips 3¾" x 76"

RED: 10 strips 2½" x 76"

SEWING DIRECTIONS

PIECING THE COLUMNS

✦ Sew red strips on each long side of the yellow strips. Make five sets.

✦ Sew green strips alternately with red and yellow sets, starting and ending with green strips.

FINISHING THE QUILT

✦ Mark a quilting design. The red and yellow bars on this quilt are over quilted with a curved feather. The green columns have a vine-and-leaf motif.

✦ Layer the quilt top, batting, and backing. Baste.

✦ Quilt and bind.

✦ Sign and date your quilt.

LANCASTER MENNONITE BARS (67" x 75½"), MAKER UNKNOWN, C. 1915, QUILTED BY TRECIA SPENCER, LUBBOCK, TEXAS. This quilt is from Sharon's collection. The top was purchased for the purpose of teaching about the colors and fabrics used in Pennsylvania. The quilting designs chosen are typical of the early 1900s – vine-and-leaf and curved-feather designs.

QUILTING DESIGN

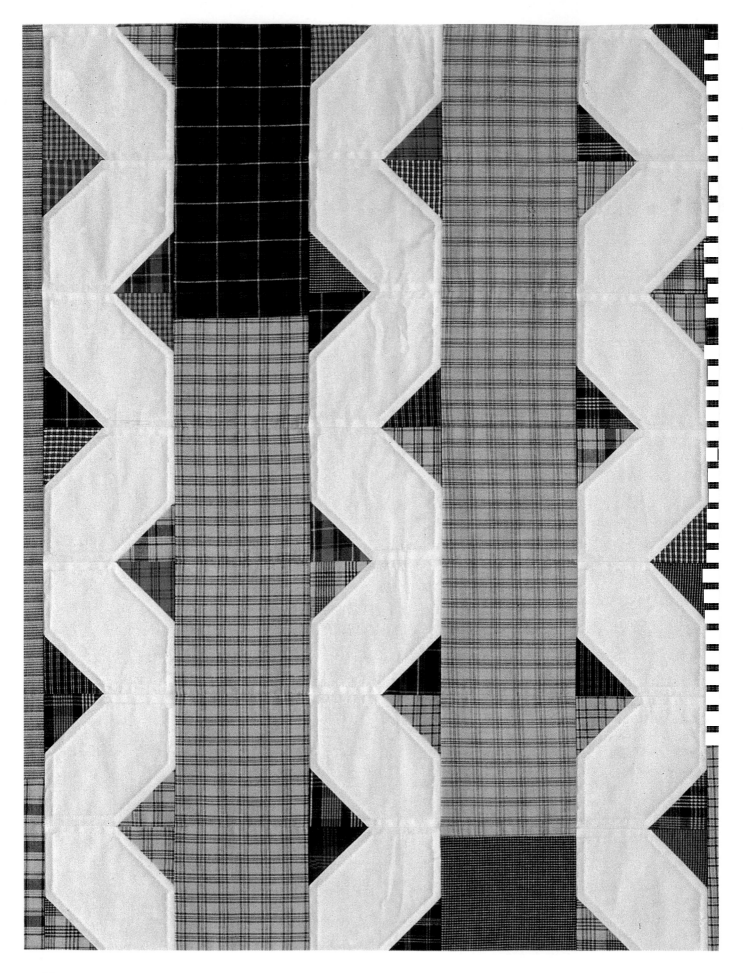

MORE VERTICAL QUILTS WITH STYLE – BOBBIE A. AUG & SHARON NEWMAN

Plaid

Quilt size 40½" x 54"
Block size 4½" x 4½"

FABRIC REQUIREMENTS

MUSLIN:

⅞ yard

SASHING, BORDERS, TRIANGLES, BINDING:

2 yards of assorted plaids

BACKING:

2⅝ yards (seam horizontally)

CUTTING LIST

MUSLIN:

40 squares 5" x 5"

PLAIDS:

2 strips 5" wide of assorted plaids to
   equal 41" for top and bottom borders
5 strips 5" wide of assorted plaids to
   equal 45½" for side borders and sashing
80 squares 2½" x 2½"

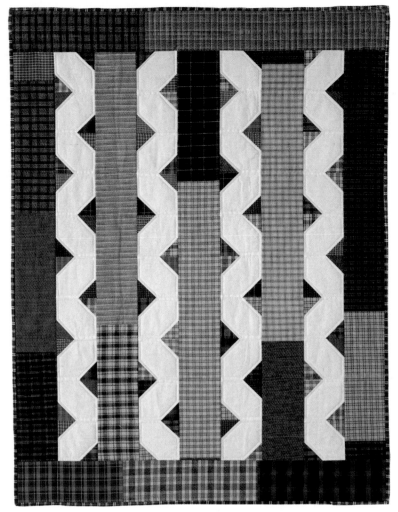

PLAID (41½" x 53½"), MADE BY BARBARA F. SHIE, COLORADO SPRINGS, COLORADO. This quilt was designed by Barbara as a presentation signature quilt. The blocks provide ample space for signatures and sayings, which would make this quilt a very special gift.

SEWING DIRECTIONS

PIECING THE COLUMNS

✦ Place plaid squares on the corners of a muslin square as shown. Draw a diagonal line from the lower right to the upper left corners of the plaid squares (Figure 1).

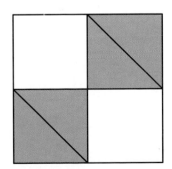

FIGURE 1. Draw diagonal lines on the plaid squares.

Plaid

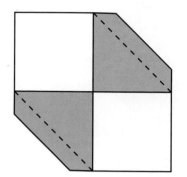

FIGURE 2. Stitch on the marked lines and trim the corners.

◆ Stitch on the marked lines. Trim the corners, leaving a ¼" seam allowance (Figure 2). Press corners open. Make 40 blocks.

◆ Sew 10 blocks into four vertical columns, alternating blocks as shown in the photograph.

ASSEMBLING THE QUILT TOP

◆ Sew the 5" strips of assorted plaids together to equal 41" for the top and bottom borders and 45½" for the side borders and sashing.

◆ Mark the sashing strips ¼" from the edge at each corner and at 4½" intervals.

◆ Arrange the columns and sashing strips, beginning and ending with a sashing strip. Pin and sew the columns and sashing strips, matching the marked points with seams. Press.

◆ Add the top and bottom pieced-plaid border strips.

FINISHING THE QUILT

◆ Mark a quilting design. A plaid grid was machine quilted in the outline of the borders. The muslin areas were quilted by the piece. The blocks are emphasized with horizontal lines quilted across the sashing strips, parallel to the block seams.

◆ Layer the quilt top, batting, and backing. Baste.

◆ Quilt and bind.

◆ Sign and date your quilt.

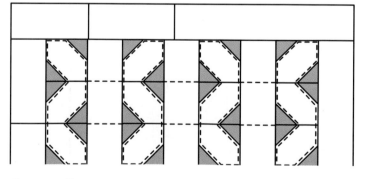

QUILTING DESIGN

Resources

MAKING HALF-SQUARE TRIANGLE UNITS
Quick Quarter Tool™
Quilter's Rule
817 Mohr Avenue
Waterford, WI 53185
(262) 514-3000

Bias Square™
Martingale & Co.
P.O. Box 118
Bothell, WA 98041
(425) 483-3313

LADY BIRD'S ROSE GARDEN
Darlene C. Christopherson
496 Bend of the Bosque Road
China Spring, TX 76633
(254) 836-1790
24-hour fax: (254) 836-1357
website: www.darlenechristopherson.com
E-mail: dcpatterns@aol.com

ADDITIONAL MATERIALS:
Appliqué Needles – Richard Hemming
    and Sons Milliners #11
Art Pencil – Verithin
Cotton Thread – Mettler 60/2
Fine Silk Pins – IBC

About the Authors

Together, Sharon and Bobbie have traveled to quilt shows, presented programs, judged quilts, taught classes, presented lectures, appraised quilts, and written four books. The co-authored titles include STRING QUILTS WITH STYLE, VERTICAL QUILTS WITH STYLE, CHARM QUILTS WITH STYLE, and MORE VERTICAL QUILTS WITH STYLE. Bobbie and Sharon have appeared on SIMPLY QUILTS with Alex Anderson and have written several articles for quilting magazines. As quilt historians, they have been invited to consult for museums, organizations, and individuals regarding their quilt collections. Their experiences as quilt appraisers have afforded them the pleasure of examining some of the most exciting antique and contemporary quilts in existence.

Please feel free to contact Sharon or Bobbie for appraisal, lecture, and workshop information.

Sharon L. Newman
P.O. Box 94594
Lubbock, TX 79493-4594
vpsln@ttu.edu

Bobbie A. Aug
P.O. Box 9414
Colorado Springs, CO 80907
qwltpro@uswest.net

Other AQS Books

This is only a small selection of the books available from the American Quilter's Society. AQS books are known worldwide for timely topics, clear writing, beautiful color photos, and accurate illustrations and patterns. The following books are available from your local bookseller, quilt shop, or the public library.

#5587   US **$18.95**

CHARM QUILTS
WITH STYLE
BOBBIE A. AUG & SHARON NEWMAN

#5710   US **$19.95**

String Quilts with Style

Bobbie Aug & Sharon Newman

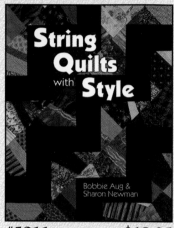

#5211   US **$18.95**

MAQS Quilts: The Founders Collection

#5883   US **$24.95**

Combing through your SCRAPS

Karen Combs

#5759   US **$19.95**

Cutting CURVES from STRAIGHT PIECES

Debbie Bowles

#5755   US **$21.95**

QUILTS FOR CHOCOLATE LOVERS

Janet Jones Worley

#5758   US **$19.95**

SCRAPS Organized to Perfection

DeLoa Jones

#6007   US **$22.95**

Dazzling STARS
A GALAXY OF BLOCK PATTERNS

Victoria Stuart & Carleen Parlato

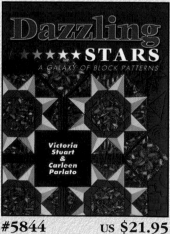

#5844   US **$21.95**

Look for these books nationally or call **1-800-626-5420**